"I ended the reading of this book deeply encouraged. The author distills the answers to those shy but pressing questions about prayer that dwell in our hearts. Deep encouragement comes from the fact that as we read we also recognize that most of the answers were inside us all along! ... Catherine's writings are refreshing because she draws generously and strikingly from her vast life experience to support her statements. Her style makes her thought accessible because she writes out of love. *Soul of My Soul* is blessed with the author's warm personal outreach that leaves the reader greatly encouraged to pray."

—*The Bread of Life*

"Recommended for every believer who wishes to grow in personal prayer."

—*National Bulletin on Liturgy*

"This is not a book to study. It is one to meditate on, to come back to again and again as a reminder that prayer is relationship... Doherty speaks in images that are more mysterious than anthropomorphic. As I read this book, I resonated with her perceptions on prayer... I also thought of others with whom I would like to share the book—persons who are struggling to find space in their lives to wrestle through deep vocational questions. I would recommend this book to them, because it might help to draw them more fully into the mystery of being a pray-er in our day."

—*Provident Book Finder*

"Catherine's writing is very simple and down to earth. This book would be appreciated by anyone searching for spiritual reading or encouragement to grow in the life of prayer. The work is well done as it contains both commentary and some of her own personal prayers that she composed. Some of them are worth framing. This is a very worthwhile book that could easily be chosen for a gift."

—Fr. Steven Palsa, *Pittsburgh Catholic*

"This book is profoundly simple, eminently personal... Catherine leads us into the spirit of her prayer after years of reflection on Eastern and Western spiritual masters."

—*Catholic Campus Ministry Association*

"A book that can be read from cover to cover or used as a help for meditation."

—*Today's Catholic*

"The heart of Catherine Doherty's thoughts on prayer are presented here in a captivating way... her words give evidence of deep spirituality and practical mysticism... She has her own distinctive style, her own particular call. Her prayer, drawn from the Christian mystical tradition of the East, has been molded amid many trials and tribulations... Overall, the combined force and wisdom of Catherine's words constitute a way of enlightened prayer for love and service in today's world."

—*Spiritual Book News*

"Written in a pratical and personal style... a fine source of reflection."

—*Today's Catholic Teacher*

"Catherine Doherty unites the Eastern Christian spirit, humbly glorifying God in contemplative prayer, with the practical Western outlook of the call for repentance... Its heart is the call to silent love of God, to simplicity in prayer, to loving regard for Jesus himself.... It will help less experienced people to begin to seek the Lord."

—*Mississippi Today*

"Suitable for any age from junior high school on into senior age. Excellent for gift-giving or lending to a friend."

—*The New Freeman*

Soul of My Soul

Coming to the Heart of Prayer

Catherine Doherty

Madonna House Publications
Combermere, Ontario, Canada

Imprimatur:
+Richard William Smith, S.T.D.
Bishop of Pembroke
August 6, 2006

Theological Censor:
Rev. John Burchat

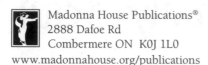 Madonna House Publications®
2888 Dafoe Rd
Combermere ON K0J 1L0
www.madonnahouse.org/publications

Soul of My Soul: Coming to the Heart of Prayer
by Catherine de Hueck Doherty (née Kolyschkine)
© 2006 Madonna House Publications. All rights reserved.

Second Revised Edition

First printing, August 15, 2006—Feast of the Assumption

Printed in Canada

Edited by Martin Nagy

Scripture quotations are taken from the *New Jerusalem Bible*, copyright
© 1985 by Darton, Longman & Todd, London, and Doubleday, a divi-
sion of Random House, Inc., New York. Quotations from Psalms are
taken from *The Psalms*, copyright © 1966 by Paulist Press, New York.

Design by Rob Huston

This book is set in Berkeley Oldstyle, designed by Frederic W. Goudy for the
University of California Press in 1938.

Library and Archives Canada Cataloguing in Publication

Doherty, Catherine de Hueck, 1896–1985.
    Soul of my soul : coming to the heart of prayer / Catherine de
Hueck Doherty.

    First ed. published Notre Dame, Ind. : Ave Maria Press, c1985
under title: Soul of my soul : reflections from a life of prayer.
    ISBN 0-921440-97-9

    1. Prayer—Catholic Church. 2. Prayer—Meditations. I. Title

BV210.2.D6 2006   248.3'2   C2006-902119-8

To my son, George DeHueck

Father, I abandon myself into your hands.
Do with me what you will.
Whatever you may do, I thank you.
I am ready for all. I accept all.
Let only your will be done in me and in all your creatures.
I wish no more than this, O Lord.
I commend my soul into your hands, for I love you, Lord,
and so need to give myself to you,
to surrender myself into your hands
without reserve and with boundless confidence,
for are my Father.

—*Blessed Charles de Foucauld*

My heart said of you, "Seek his face."
Lord, I do seek your face;
do not hide your face from me....
You are my help.
Lord, teach me your way,
lead me in the path of integrity....
I believe I shall see the goodness of the Lord
in the land of the living.
Put your hope in the Lord, be strong, let your heart be bold.

—*Psalm 27:8–14*

Contents

Introduction

Thousands of books have been written on prayer. I don't suppose God minds the books, but I think he wants you and me to be the book. He wants us to be the word. He wants us to reflect his face. How do we do that? We pray.

Prayer is so very simple. Many people think it is something esoteric, as if you could only learn to pray after having studied theology and spirituality and the different methodologies of prayer, from St. Teresa of Avila to transcendental meditation. I think that if Christ had wanted to talk to Ph.D.s, he would have found their equivalent in the society of his day. Why did Jesus become a carpenter and not a rabbi? He talked to Peter and John. He talked to illiterate people, and they absorbed his voice and understood his words because he spoke so simply.

If you want to know what prayer is like, listen to a child of two or three speaking. When I address God in a childlike way, that's a prayer.

When I fall in love with someone and we begin, slowly, shyly, reticently, to explore each other's lives, as lovers do, that's a prayer. When we have become husband and wife and entered into the fullness of our love in the great sacrament of matrimony, we experience the tremendous silence of a unity that is both physical and spiritual. That silence is a prayer.

Loneliness is a prayer. Every man and woman, married or single, in every vocation, is lonely. When that terrible loneliness comes upon us, a cry wells up deep in our heart like the cry of a mute person and rises to God. That is a prayer.

How can you define prayer, except by saying that it is love? It is love expressed in speech and love expressed in silence. To put it another way, prayer is the meeting of two loves—the love of God and the love of his child. That's all there is to prayer.

Falling in Love with God

I hear my Beloved knocking. "Open to me."

Song of Songs 5:2

Why should it be difficult to fall in love with God?

The Lord speaks to us in the Old Testament, although you have prostituted yourselves under every bush, come back to me, Israel (Hosea 4:12,13;14:2), and "Though your sins are like scarlet, they shall be as white as snow" (Isaiah 1:18). The Lord is the bridegroom of Israel; she is his spouse. Christ speaks to us about being the bridegroom. The Psalms speak of him leaping over the hills to come to his beloved. The Song of Songs says, "Let him kiss me with the kisses of his mouth." (Song of Songs 1:2)

If all of this is true (and it is), what's the matter with us? Why do we have to inquire about how to pray? Perhaps, we are really asking about how to love. After all, prayer is simply an expression of our love.

We contemplate God as two lovers contemplate one another. They hold hands and look deep into one another's eyes. Prayer is like a woman contemplating her husband after the marriage act. Both lie still and gaze upon each other in silence.

Silence is the greatest expression of love. Such silence is deep, unfathomable, and endless. Such silence partakes already of eternity. Such silence touches the face of God, upon whom without God's grace, man cannot gaze and live. This kind of silence embraces Christ, touches

11

the face of the Father, and knows by experience the reality of the Holy Spirit.

At first, such a silence is tremulous, because it is difficult for us to rid ourselves of extraneous thoughts. Little by little, the silence becomes quiet, and the person, with hands extended or with no gestures at all, loses himself slowly into God. Or rather, God draws you into himself until everything is totally still. Then, we know God is present. This silence becomes the moment when the kingdom of heaven is present among us. Such is the knowledge we receive in the darkness of unknowing, where God teaches man about himself and about other people.

Prayer is simple. We repeat the name of our Beloved: "Jesus, Jesus, Jesus." We call this "the prayer of the presence of God." The person who has closed the window of his intellect and opened the door of his heart, the person who has gone into the depths of silence, returns with the name of God upon his lips and in his heart. Now, he goes about the world repeating it, and in this way he becomes a prayer. A person achieves great joy when he becomes a prayer. Wherever he goes, he radiates Christ.

Christ says, "If you love those who love you, what right have you to claim any credit? Even the pagans do as much" (Matthew 5:46,48). I might dislike somebody, but love is greater than that. The ability to overcome a dislike is part of our human greatness. It makes me more than simply human; it makes me supernatural if I do it in the name of love. Out of love, St. Francis kissed the leper. Such love has no walls, no frontiers. It is as infinite as eternity, as immense as God. There is no limit to God. This kind of love encompasses all creation.

Prayer will come when we fall in love with God. The way to fall in love with him is on our knees. Everything in us resists this falling in love. Who wants to fall in love with the Crucified One? Who wants to climb the hill of Golgotha, eternally present to all of us? Who wants to be crucified on the other side of Christ's cross, even though this is his wedding bed? If we fall in love with the Crucified One, we shall know joy beyond all knowing. We shall have peace, the peace he promised. We shall be able to lift up all things before his face.

We shall make up for what is wanting in the sufferings of Christ, for the body of Christ still suffers. Our prayer today should be like this, "Lord, I love you for those who love you not. Lord, I love you for those who love you not," repeated over and over again.

If we reach this point, prayer will spring like a song from our heart. Love will uphold it. Once we fall in love with God, we will love even if we don't necessarily like the untrustworthy, the ugly, the tired, the sick, the drug addict, the murderer, everyone. When we fall in love with God, we will receive the gift of compassion and of tenderness, for God himself is compassion and tenderness. With these gifts, we will begin to be people of the towel and water, washing the feet of everyone, because we know that everyone is Christ and Christ is in everyone.

"At night...I will rise...I will seek him whom my heart loves," says the Song of Songs. (3:1, 2 RSV) Suddenly, I encounter him. He is here. Now, everyone around me becomes my beloved. Now, it is easy for me to love. Prayer pours forth from my heart as simply as a brook runs down to a river. Prayer is simply love gushing toward the Beloved.

I Prayed

I prayed to God for songs and laughter. He gave me tears instead. I prayed for life in valleys green, full of harvest rich. He led me through deserts arid and heights where snow alone could feel at home. I prayed for sun, lots of dancing, and sparkling rivers to sail upon. He gave me night, quite dark, starless, and thirst to guide me through its wastes.

But now I know that I was foolish, for I have more than I prayed for. I have the Son for bridegroom. The music of his voice is a valley green and river sparkling on which I sail. My soul is dancing, dancing with endless joy in the dark night he shares with me.

A Risky Business

"Father," he said, "if you are willing, take this cup away from me. Nevertheless, let your will be done, not mine."

Luke 22:42

In his book, *Living Prayer*, Archbishop Anthony Bloom writes, "The experience of prayer can only be known from the inside and is not to be dallied with."

From many books, one gets the impression that we should learn to pray because prayer is so interesting and thrilling, that it is the discovery of a new world where one meets God and finds the way to spiritual life. That's true—but the implications of prayer are more far-reaching than that. Prayer is an adventure, but it is a dangerous one. We cannot enter into it without risk. "It is a fearful thing to fall into the hands of the living God" (Hebrews 10:31 RSV).

At Madonna House, our experience with the poustinia[1], and with the questions people ask, has shown us that we can't speak of prayer as if it were some new fad everyone should try. Prayer must lead us to total surrender, or it will lead us nowhere except back to ourselves.

It is this surrender that we fear. Following Christ is indeed a risky business. He calls us to enter a revolution. Not like the Russian revolution or the Cuban revolution, but one that is infinitely more powerful. This revolution

---

1. "Poustinia" is the Russian word for "desert" and signifies a room where one goes alone to fast and pray for twenty-four hours or more. See the book *Poustinia: Encountering God in Silence, Solitude and Prayer* published by Madonna House, 2000.

takes place inside of us, for heaven is taken by violence to oneself. Do not fool yourself: once you encounter God, you will no longer be the same person you were before.

How do we go to God in prayer? The answer appears in the beginning of St. Matthew's Gospel: The Magi saw the long-expected star. First of all, they believed. Secondly, they set out without delay. They didn't sit around discussing the matter. Thirdly, they found the King, and when they arrived at the manger, they knelt, they worshipped, and they presented their gifts. They contemplated Christ and adored him. This is the essence of prayer.

The Price of Souls

Is this the price one must pay for souls that have gone astray? Is this the coin of love meted out like drops of blood falling on stone one by one, hot, red, each one brought forth in labor and in pain? If this be so, then for one soul, Beloved, take all of me. Forgive my tears, for I am weak. But for a soul I'll stand here, a lamb, as meek as you.

Holding the Hand of God

I found him whom my heart loves.
I held him fast, nor would I let him go.

Song of Songs 3:4

Hold the hand of the Lord, and talk to him any time you wish.

There is not a time to pray and a time not to pray. To pray is to pray always. You hold the hand of God. Sometimes you talk to him, sometimes you don't, but you are with him all the time.

We don't need to spend all our time on our knees—we need to serve each other. Of course, we need to pray, but we can pray in our heart, constantly and without ceasing. Always you are offering up prayer for others, and in doing so, you're in touch with the whole world in a beautiful and wondrous way.

When a mother is busy with her children, an employee with his job, a missionary with the poor, they may think they have no time to pray. That isn't true. You give your time to everyone and everything, but in your heart, you pray continuously. You know that the Lord is near and that he holds your hand while you go about your business.

Prayer is simply the communication that constantly passes between you and the Lord. Prayer is conversation with him. You don't need to understand how you talk to God. You just do it. He loves to listen to you and especially delights in your silence when you listen to him. Most of us are not used to praying as life flows along. We're used to "taking time" for prayer. In truth, we should be praying all the time. Prayer never stops.

We can go into God's heart simply and directly, loving him, knocking at his door, and saying, "Lord, please let me in. I love you. You're so important to me." Quietly and slowly, we begin to understand what he is saying, and our lives begin to change. Everything becomes different. We listen and listen. God's words pass through our brains and into our innermost selves. We begin to know what it means to belong to God and to love him, to be his very own.

Listen to him. What he has to say is vitally important for us. Hold onto him with all your might and let everything else fall away. Nothing is of much importance compared to God. When he becomes the center of our life, all else will settle into place.

We want to get to know God. Once we start talking with him, we begin to know him. Slowly, his will becomes our will. Prayer is the entry into God's heart. It is the opening of one's heart to God. Throughout the day, you talk to God. You find out what he wants, and when, and how. He guides you in every way. He wants a friend. He wants you to share with him how you think about him, and if you listen, he will tell you more and more about himself.

People come to me and say, "How does one pray in the city?" Prayer comes from the heart, not because of this place or that. Your heart is with you all the time. You can't separate it from yourself. Prayer is a question of interiorization. The same is true of the poustinia. Is a poustinia one of our log cabins at Madonna House? Is it a room? Is it a particular building? It is your heart. You enter into your heart and there you visit God.

In the city or in the country, on the railroad, in a car, on a steamboat or an airplane, mining the bowels of the earth, working all day, sweeping, cleaning, lecturing, talking, my heart can he attentive to God. You speak and your heart is with God. Even while you sleep, your heart is with him. As the scriptures say, "I sleep, but my heart is awake" (Song of Songs 5:2).

Prayer is standing still before God. If you get all excited about how you're going to stand still, you certainly aren't going to be very still. Ask yourself the question, "How peaceful is my mind, my soul, my heart, when I turn my face to God? Am I listening to the noise of my own self, or am I listening to God?" We stand still before God and wait for the Holy Spirit.

The Jesus prayer, "Lord Jesus Christ, Son of the Living God, have mercy on me, a sinner," is a good beginning. From it other prayer will come.

Do you understand what it means to be close to God? It is such joy. Hold on to this joy, keep it with you, and preach the gospel with your life. Preach the gospel with your whole heart, your whole mind, and your whole soul. Preach it. It is the only thing that matters.

It is not enough to pray prayers. You have to go deeply within yourself. Prayer is the ultimate reality of my life. It is my relationship with God and with mankind. It is time we stand close to God in some visible way, so that others, seeing us, may also hold on to the hand of God. When people know we are close to God, our words and our life take on new meaning for them. They follow us to the source of what they most deeply desire themselves.

The life of a Christian is a prayer. We are like diamonds, shining in many different ways. Each facet has been polished by God. Our very being renders glory to him. The simple fact that we are baptized in the death and resurrection of Christ is enough to make us a prayer. Sweeping, washing, cleaning, serving our families in small ways—all this is prayer. Studying is a prayer, if this is what we are supposed to be doing. Being sick is a prayer; being healthy is a prayer. I can't imagine any aspect of a Christian life that is not a facet of this sparkling diamond.

We cannot understand this through our intellect. Prayer makes sense only when we pray, only in the context of an ongoing relationship with God, for it is he who has fashioned this many-faceted diamond out of his infinite love. Love begets love. For this we have been created: that we might become one with God. He doesn't place obstacles in our path but throws open the road that leads to this union. The path is narrow but the horizons are immense.

There are times specifically allotted for prayer. The Mass is the prayer of prayers, the moment in the day when my union with Christ is concrete. I eat God. I drink God. In a mysterious way—which I call mystical—he and I are one, the Bridegroom of my soul is also the Bridegroom of my body. You don't really pray the Mass; you experience it. It encompasses you totally and absolutely. In some profound sense, you become the Mass. The Mass is your daily rendezvous with God. It's important that you be there. Between two Masses—the Mass of today and the Mass of tomorrow—you spend your time talking lovingly to God. I like the Liturgy of the Hours—the psalms and readings come from scripture, the word of God. One can pray before the Blessed Sacrament or in the privacy of one's room. One can make days of poustinia. The Way of the Cross, the rosary, the Akathist of the Eastern Church, the prayers that Christians say across the world in every rite are all beautiful and should be part of our lives.

One of the greatest prayers is the prayer of forgiveness. The examination of conscience is one of the best moments of any day. You look the day over and examine yourself from the only point of view that matters: charity. If you have not forgiven someone, if you have rejected or been nasty to someone and apologies are required, make sure you do so the next day. A sin is a sin, and like a grain of sand in my shoe, it rubs. Apologize to God for all sins, great and small. Say you're sorry. Every moment is the moment of beginning again.

O Jesus

O Jesus, I want you to be loved by all, passionately, especially by Christians. You are so beautiful. You are the Lord. Give us the grace to love you and make you loved by all we meet.

On Becoming a Prayer

Planted in love and built on love, you will with all the
saints have strength to grasp the breadth and the length,
the height and the depths; until, knowing the love of
Christ, which is beyond all knowledge, you are filled
with the utter fullness of God.

Ephesians 3:17–19

People ask me how I pray. It's hard to answer such questions, but I do my best because I know that "prayer is a hunger," in the words of Fr. Edward Farrell, and my brothers and sisters are as hungry for it as I am.

I fell in love with God when I was six. God was close to me in the same way that a child is close to another child. Since I have a vivid imagination, we did a lot of things together. We even played ball. I wanted to share my food with him until I found out I couldn't. But God continued to be my friend.

I proceeded slowly, painstakingly, to vocal prayers. Those fell away, and I found myself in a new land—meditation. I compare it to going to a dance and finding a boyfriend who attracts you deeply. You remember and savor every word he says. My lover was Christ, and so I read the gospel avidly, meditating on each word. The Gospel became my favorite prayer.

Meditation fell away as old clothes, and now I was clad in the beautiful garments of contemplation. Life was entirely different. It seemed as if the Lord himself were explaining things to me. In meditation, my intellect had sought the answers. Now God himself clarified this or that passage. I was lost in God in those days.

Where does one go after being "lost in God"? You will not be able to understand it with your head but only with your heart. What happened was I myself became a prayer.

A person who is a prayer is someone deeply in love with the Word, deeply in love with a Person. When you are in love with God, your head is plunged into your heart. It is the happiest time of your life. Of course, we use our minds as far as practical needs are concerned. The house gets cleaned. The duty of the moment is always there. Far from interfering with your life, being a prayer makes you meticulous about doing little things well for the love of God. The detached, critical part of your brain that endlessly dissects and analyzes and rationalizes about matters of faith has gone into your heart. This is what it means to become a prayer.

Prayer is suffering. It is "com-passion" (suffering with). Out of nowhere, the suffering of humanity will fill you and you are like one dead. You listen to the news, and you are the man who has been kidnapped by terrorists. You become the woman dying of cancer. The pain of the whole world is upon you. At this moment, you don't pray. You simply share the suffering. That is what it means to be a prayer.

From another corner of the earth, you hear good news. You hear of a fiesta being celebrated, and you share the happiness. Suddenly you feel like dancing in the middle of the night. You feel that perhaps God is dancing with you.

Sometimes you're empty. You look at yourself and say, "What am I doing here?" You feel as if you're no good. Temptations assail you, and a thousand tongues of doubt lick you like flames. That is when you become a prayer for the doubtful.

Sometimes you go into the depths of hell, a man-made hell, an atheistic hell where you can't move. You are the atheist. But you descend there of your own free will, out of love. Your identification is a prayer.

Prayer is a movement, an impetus of the heart. Three-quarters of your life you'll feel as if you cannot pray. Of course, you cannot pray! Who do you think you are, an angel who can say to God for all eternity, "Glory, glory, glory"? It is impossible to pray the way you think you should pray.

Prayer is being constantly in the presence of God. You are led to it. The poustinia will lead you faster. Suddenly, you know he is always there. You can't pray? He sits there and doesn't mind at all. He prays for you (Romans 8:26).

As you pray about the living, the suffering, the doubting, and all these things, God is there. Once he is there, all things are there, and you become a prayer. When you have become a prayer, you will be ready to be crucified. No one has the strength to be crucified unless it is given to him by God, and God will give that strength to those who, clothing the gospel with their flesh, become a prayer before his Face.

Here we begin to touch the mystery of the Incarnation. It is the mystery of ordinariness, of the commonplace, of the obvious. It is the mystery of love. What is more ordinary than a baby born in a cave in Palestine where many people lived in caves? What is more commonplace than to go into a cave like that when all the inns are full? It was the obvious thing to do.

We can follow Christ's Incarnation into our humanity step by step, and at each step, the mystery of the ordinary, the commonplace, and the obvious will hit us like a sledgehammer. He has taken upon himself our life—ordinary, commonplace, and obvious—and our mystery. But by incarnating himself in our flesh, he has made us more mysterious than we had been before his coming. He has divinized our ordinary, commonplace existence through his Incarnation.

The mystery of God becoming man and of man "becoming God" meet in prayer: the prayer of the Son to the Father and of man to his Brother. By his Incarnation, the God-man was able to pray to the Father and, by our divinization in Christ, we are able to pray through Jesus Christ to God the Father. God and man are thus united in prayer, joined in the one prayer which is Jesus Christ. In him, man, too, becomes a prayer.

The key is the acceptance of the ordinary, the commonplace, and the obvious, all of which, since the Resurrection of the Lord Jesus, are radiant with the glory of God.

Look at the sacraments. Take baptism, so very commonplace in the Christian world. A child. Water. Oil. Cotton. A priest. Godparents. All very tangible, very obvious, and yet, who has plumbed the depths of this sacrament? Who has considered what it really means to be baptized into the death and resurrection of Jesus Christ?

Confirmation is the reality of being possessed by the Spirit. We enter that reality as baptized children of God. "I am sending down to you what the Father has promised. Stay in the city then, until you are clothed with the power from on high" (Luke 24:49). Do you realize what happened? He told them of the power with which they were going to be clothed and with which we too are clothed in the sacrament of confirmation. This power was not only given to the apostles, it is given to you and me. It deepens our mystery, for we are men and women of glory and power, provided we understand the obvious and the commonplace.

The ability to understand the ordinariness in these boundless mysteries can be achieved only by faith and our acceptance of Christ's law of love. It is not enough to believe it in our minds and confess it with our tongues. It must be incarnated. We must clothe it with our flesh, preaching the Gospel with our very lives. Only then will we be men and women who have a key to our own mystery and God's.

We will become more fully a prayer, for prayer is born when the mystery of God and the mystery of man meet. This power and glory are given to us that we might daily become more like Christ, that we daily become the way to the Father. This power and glory are given to us that we might realize we are brothers and sisters of Christ and that we, too, have been sent to do the will of the Father and, thus, to lead people to him. The power and the mystery entrusted to us is given that we might say, "It is no longer I who live, but Christ who lives in me" (Galatians 2:20 RSV). That is our power. That is our glory. That is our mystery.

They Ask Me How I Pray

They ask me often how I pray. What can I tell them, Lord, who am myself your most unprofitable servant? How could I tell that first I lay prostrated in the dust, the mud of all the roads you made me walk? Where are the words that could explain those lonely roads, their gray, dry dust, and black, black, mud? How could I tell how dark the days, how cold the nights upon these roads? How to explain that all I saw on all these endless roads everywhere were green, rough trees, and you stretched out upon them, dying?

Where are the words to tell that when you took me off those thousand lonely roads, and sent me forth into the haunts of men, I wept; for then I knew my poverty and theirs, and so I wept and wept for my sins and theirs, and for your unrequited love of us.

Perhaps you'll give me words today to tell that now I know, and I praise you for every-thing—the thousand roads, their black mud and gray, gray dust, their numbing pain, the gift of tears, the sight of poverty. But most of all, I praise you for every tree I saw, green and rough, and you dying on them of love for us.

The Shepherd's Flute

"Did not our hearts burn within us as he talked to us
on the road and explained the scriptures to us?"

Luke 24:32

Have you ever heard a shepherd's flute in Scotland, or
in Jerusalem? It is so haunting, so enticing, so irresistible that you have to follow the sound and go see where
it comes from. The Good Shepherd's flute is constantly
playing. If we close our ears to it, life will be miserable
indeed. Madonna House is really an apostolate of music.
We are listening to the Shepherd's flute, of which all music is but an echo.

The story of Madonna House Apostolate is the story
of prayer. Everything that happens to us involves prayer.
Ours is the story of two words, "*fiat*" and "alleluia." To say
fiat is to say yes to God, and this yes is often painful.

We cannot live these words without constant prayer. It
is inconceivable to think we can live them by ourselves,
but this has always been mankind's greatest temptation.
Throughout the ages, we have tried to build our Tower of
Babel that we might reach up to heaven (Genesis 11:1–9).
Every day, every moment, we have polished the same
old apple that we might become like God (Genesis 3:4,5).
Because of this strange tendency embedded in our fallen
human nature, it is imperative that we, as Christians,
hear and put into practice the words of Christ, "Cut off
from me you can do nothing" (John 15:5).

These words, spoken two thousand years ago, have still not penetrated our hearts. We are reluctant to accept them. "No!" we protest. "It isn't true! I can do a lot of things without you—just watch me. I can earn your approval, your grace, your salvation—you don't have to give me gifts all the time. I don't want to recognize you as the creator of everything. I want to put in my own two cents worth."

We can contribute our own "two cents worth" and more, provided we realize that nothing is possible without God. Once we recognize this, we can give him a million dollars. As St. Paul says, we can make up what is wanting in the sufferings of Christ (Colossians 1:24). We can "wait on the Lord" (Psalm 37). We can allow the idea of total dependence to permeate our life until, like sugar dissolved in boiling water, the two become indistinguishable.

Prayer is my total faith in God as my creator. I am his image, his icon, and without him, I can do nothing. Prayer is my recognition of who I really am: a saved sinner, capable of breaking my friendship with God at any given moment and even likely to revel in its breaking. When I recognize this, prayer becomes a basic necessity for my life.

There is a strange, inexplicable restlessness that we all have felt at one time or another. We have restless feet, restless hearts, hearts that are angry and disturbed, hearts that reject the other, hearts that seek but never find. Praise be to God if we continue to search, but too often we are satisfied with less than the real desire of our hearts.

What is it, fundamentally, that we all seek?

Be careful not to confuse this yearning with the desires for sex and marriage. Sex is powerful and marriage is a wonderful vocation for those called to it, but, basically, this is not what we are looking for. This sidetracks us and confuses the issue. We think that union with another will lead us to union with God. It's possible, if it is God's will for you to be married, but don't kid yourself that marriage will automatically lead you to God. You have to go through the same travail of the spirit, the same dispossession and death to self as you would if you were single, a priest or a nun, or in any other vocation.

There is no shortcut to union with God, unless God himself provides it. Once in a while he does. Sometimes he literally pounces on a soul. St. Germaine, an uneducated shepherdess, is one example; St. Bernadette Soubirous is another. God can work in any way he pleases. Normally, however, we have to walk the road to union with God. He is the only one who can quench our thirst and still our restlessness.

Prayer is the passionate desire of a human being to become one with God. It is the slow discovery that in order to reach this union, one must be dispossessed of his very self. There is a deep mystery to all this, and I am not good at probing mysteries. I wait for God to explain them, if he so wishes, or else I accept them without explanation. Patience is the key.

Day after day, hour after hour, we come to realize the price of this union with God. The images of courtship and marriage in the Bible warn us of this, for love and marriage inevitably bring pain. We don't often think of it that way, but so it is. I fall in love with someone I didn't even know existed three months ago, and now I'm worried because he's driving to Chicago and it's raining. Before I knew this fellow, I was peaceful, but the moment I entered into a love relationship with him, the pain began. I didn't have to wait until I married him.

Suppose you get married. You are full of beautiful dreams. Then you become pregnant. You vomit every morning, you can't make dinner, you get disgusted with the whole situation. Of course, you're happy you're going to have a child, but today, you're downright miserable. Eventually, the child is born. For two years, he screams and cries. You haven't got the money for a babysitter, so you can't go out with your husband. You're tied down and shut in and for your efforts you get "Mwah! Mwah!" You love the baby, but you wish he were in kindergarten. When he gets to kindergarten, you're worried sick about him crossing the street or getting measles from the other kids. When he grows up, you worry about all the things that can happen to teenagers. Then you worry about him marrying, and then you worry about his children. Love is like that.

Where there is love, there is pain. But whatever our walk in life, this kind of pain is God's way of teaching us how to pray. Everything that happens to us spiritually, everything that causes us to grow, will bring us closer to God if we say yes. Spiritual growth doesn't come from what we do, necessarily. Sometimes it comes from simply sitting and seeing the shambles of what we tried to accomplish, from watching what was seemingly God's work go to pot. You can't do anything about it but watch.

This happened to me. I knew dimly then what I see more clearly today—that this was the moment when God really picked me up and said, "Now I am offering you the union you seek. The other side of my cross is empty. Come, be nailed upon it. This is our marriage bed."

All we can answer in response to that invitation, is, "Help me, God! I don't have the courage to climb on this cross."

Not only does God give us the grace to believe and to ask for help, but he also draws us to himself. His own desire pulls us toward himself until the two desires meet. The prayer of man and the desire of God come together in one brief moment of union, which only whets our desire for more. It is an insatiable taste of what we seek, and it will give us the courage to say yes to the next devastating situation that comes along, the next stepping stone to union on the cross that the Carpenter has fashioned for each one of us individually.

Prayer is that hunger for union which never lets go of us. It beats into our blood with the very beat of our hearts. It is a thirst that can be quenched by nothing except God. It is as if one's whole body is poised on tip-toe, our hands stretching upward as if to touch the cosmos. The act of praying, like the act of love, involves movement and effort. You don't pray like a robot any more than you make love like one. Prayer is movement, stretching, seeking, holding, finding only to seek again: "I opened to my Beloved, but he had turned his back and gone!" (Song of Songs 5:6).

Prayer is walking up to an abyss, looking down, and being unable to see the bottom for there is none. You spend years balancing on the edge, almost jumping in, then retreating. At some moment, the hunger becomes too great and the thirst too flaming. You jump. You jump into the abyss, only to discover that there is no abyss, only God and the depth of his love for you. For a moment, you catch your breath in his arms. Then once again, because he loves you, he seems to elude you, so that again you might go forth to seek him.

Prayer is constant movement. Strangely enough, it is movement into oneself where the Trinity dwells. That's why dispossession has to come from within, for the obstacles that separate us from God are never outside us. "Nothing that goes into a man from outside can make him unclean; it is the things that come out of a man that make him unclean" (Mark 7:15). Dispossession is like taking a broom to one's inner being to clear out everything that keeps us from being united to God. If I ask myself what paradise is, I think it must be that recognition of the Christ who has always dwelt within me. Death will be the breaking of the barrier between myself and the indwelling Trinity. Then I shall know that I was always united with God, that he was always with me.

However, I don't have to wait for death. I am not trying to reach some distant star. As it says in the book of Deuteronomy, "It is not in heaven that you need to wonder, 'Who will go up to heaven for us and bring it down to us, so that we may hear it and keep it? Nor is it beyond the seas...No, the Word is very near to you, it is in your mouth and in your heart" (Deuteronomy 30:12–14). I can have faith that God dwells within me now. God is in me; that is why I must love myself.

Closed Doors

I beat my soul against closed doors of human hearts until my soul is but a mess of wounds. You took me to your cellars, Lord, and precious wines you gave me there to drink. It seemed to me that I was lying within the circle of your arms, resting upon your heart.

You sang of turtledoves and of love having come to our land. And then you bade me to arise and go in search of souls. "For this," you said, "I gave you the choicest wine to drink. For this, I let you hear the living love that is the beating of my heart."

So here I am, on fire, exiled from you and our land. I cannot hear the turtledove, and all is dark. Yet I know you send me into exile because you love me. Then give me strength not to glance back but to run with giant steps forward, believing that the wind of your will will carry me to the end of the earth.

I live, exist, have my being within the soundless sound of God's voice. I am encompassed, filled, and drowning in the sea of music that is his voice. It seems that I myself have become but an echo of all his songs. A troubadour am I, who wanders without zither or guitar, yet a troubadour forever singing soundless songs to all who come within hearing distance of my silent voice. How can I live and echo this sea of music—and yet be silent!

Fire and Tears

Do not let your hearts be troubled. Trust in God.

John 14:1

I often meditate on holy cards. Yesterday, I came across one that speaks of prayer as fire and tears. It seems to me that this is the content of prayer. When you ask yourself where prayer comes from, you will discover that it comes from the heart. It follows, then, that the heart must also be on fire and full of tears. I left that holy picture with another one I had found, which reads, "People who trust are the robbers of God's grace." I continued to meditate on them.

The fire is the fire of God's love. The tears are not tears of compunction, necessarily; they can be tears of gratitude. They form a river within us.

To discover this type of prayer, we must be willing to look deeply into ourselves. We will get nowhere by loitering on the surface. We must reach that level of our heart where prayer and surrender go hand in hand.

The prayer of fire and tears takes place in silence. Like all things of the heart, it happens quietly. We speak to God in our funny little way trying to tell him that we love him, that we are on fire with love for him, and that we weep in gratitude that he has come down to us. God listens and listens. He listens to us as no one else could ever do. He listens with his whole being, because he loves us so.

Sometimes our prayer doesn't reach him. It falls short because it is not rooted in reality. God created reality; he is reality; and the kind of prayer he desires from us is real prayer. Archbishop Anthony Bloom puts it well in his book, *Beginning to Pray*, "The moment we try to be what we are not, there is nothing left to say or have; we become a fictitious personality, an unreal presence, and this unreal presence cannot be approached by God."

Truth is love. We pray, but we fail to love one another. We fail to love our neighbor. We don't even love ourselves. We don't love our enemies, and we're not about to hand over our lives as martyrs. We talk and talk about these things but don't do them, and so our prayers, though they may be wet with tears and blazing with fire, fall short of God as if blocked by a brick wall.

For our prayer to be rooted in love, we must be willing to face conflicts openly. In any department of Madonna House, when people are angry with each other, they have to come together and talk it out. They must be willing to say, "Look, I am angry. This is why, and this is what is really in my heart." They also have to be willing to take the consequences of such openness. Here it may be the other person shooting the truth back: "You're angry because you want attention and no one could possibly fill the need you have." In circumstances outside Madonna House, the consequences might be much more drastic. We are called to say what we have to say without fear. Being human, we may be afraid, but we speak the truth regardless. If we do, people will not only believe us, but believe in us.

When we were trying to organize a union in the T. Eaton Company (a department store in Toronto at that time), everything was being done secretly, behind closed doors. "This is no good," I said to the other employees.

"We have to confront people directly with this situation. We can't just spring a union on them out of the blue. We have to tell them what we're doing." Predictably, I was told, "If you're so smart, you go tell them." I did, and I lost my job. Later, a union did form at the T. Eaton Company.

Throughout our lives, we will have to face things squarely. We will have to do it with our husband or wife, with our friends, with our co-workers. We will achieve nothing by trying to hide our anger. As long as we fail to confront situations as they are—acknowledging our fault when the fault is ours, or asking the other about it if he is in the wrong—there will be a world of unclarity and lack of truth between us and God.

We can hurt each other terribly, consciously or un-consciously. Why else would God tell us to love our enemies? My worst enemy may not be the Communist; it might be you. I might be your enemy. You might feel like strangling me at times. We are called to truth, and we are called to forgiveness, but we are also called to become the cross on which the other is crucified. We have to be honest about this.

"People who trust are the robbers of God's grace," reads the holy card. We have to trust each other, and we can't go around muttering in corners. Such muttering is like a knife in somebody's back, and it stops our prayer cold. It is terrible to be truthful and even more terrible to be trusting. But that is what we are called to do. We trust because God himself trusts the untrustworthy. That is obvious, because he trusts you and me.

Prayer is composed of fire and tears, and this is what we bring to God. We bring him the fire of our love and the river of our tears, those shed in the light of gratitude and those shed in the darkness of sorrow. If we live in truth, our hearts will be at peace. Our prayers, purified in the fire of truth and cleansed by tears that wash away the debris within us, will rise like incense before the face of God. We will be living and praying as Christ himself lived and prayed.

Against Peace

Faith is old, and hope is dying,
Charity's cold, selling and buying.
Who wants peace and all its arts now?
Soon may it cease, lift up your hearts now.
Ask for danger, ask for glory,
the fear and the fun,
and life like a story
in the wind and the sun.
Send us now a sudden waking,
a royal row, a thorough shaking.
For we must be sharply goaded,
our souls all rust with ink corroded.
Pray you, Lord, at end of writing,
send us a sword and a little fighting.
Send us danger, send us glory,
the fear and the fun,
and death like a story
in the wind and the sun.

The Spirit of Prayer

Our God is a consuming fire.

Hebrews 12:29

"We shall come to him and make our home with him" (John 14:23). We do not grasp the significance of these words of Christ for the daily lives of millions of people. All over the world, people are born and die each day, but who knows them? Who remembers them? The psalmist writes that the life of man is "like grass sprouting and flowering in the morning, withered and dry before dusk" (Psalm 90:5,6). What meaning do Christ's words have in their hidden, unsung lives?

"My Father and I shall come to you and make our home with you." Besides our baptism, besides the food of the Eucharist that sustains us along the way, besides the psychological assurance and the spiritual reality of forgiveness in the sacrament of Penance, what exactly do these words mean to us? Christ assures us that the Trinity dwells in us. This is the essence of faith and of our life as Christians, the starting point to be returned to again and again like a fountain of crystal clear water.

We talk about our feelings of inadequacy. We doubt ourselves. We feel we'll never achieve anything. That's not too serious. But when we see ourselves as worthless, filled with guilt, suffering from inferiority complexes no psychiatrist could ever cure, how then can we enter into ourselves and believe that God lives within us? We have to shake that guilt from ourselves like we shake out a rug.

We have to get a broom and sweep the cobwebs from our minds. God has made his abode in us. His words are clear, precise, and simple: "My Father and I will come and dwell in you." He simply says, "We will be there." God loves us, not because we are good but because he is good.

The essence of life is the Trinity dwelling in me and the journey inward deeper and deeper to the Source of all life. Whatever beautiful thoughts you have, however much inspired by the Holy Spirit, they are drops in a bucket drawn from the infinite ocean of life within you.

God is movement, God is creation, and creation is always movement. God is fire, the fire of love. God is wind, the wind of the Holy Spirit coming down on the apostles. He is not a destructive wind but one that cleanses us from the oppressive heat, that picks us up and carries us from one place to another. All this is symbolic. We say that the Trinity is fire and wind and movement because "Trinity" is a concept that we can never understand with our minds. We can only enter into its mystery, into the heart of the flame, into the eye of the whirlwind, by the grace of Jesus Christ, the second person of the Trinity.

Daily we enter the Trinity through our journey inward. There I find the God who dwells in my heart. Immediately, I open wide my arms to embrace my brother with this renewed life. I touch God, I touch you, and I am cruciform as a Christian is meant to be. I pick you up and bring you with me, not into myself but upwards. I lift you up to the Trinity.

Tolstoy has a beautiful story about the prayer to the Trinity.[2] A Russian bishop was making a visitation of his diocese. In that diocese was a forgotten island to which

---

2. "The Three Hermits" by Leo Tolstoy.

no one ever went. When the bishop heard that three hermits dwelt there, he felt obliged to go see them. After all, they were under his care. Arriving at the island, he found three old men who kept repeating, "Three are thee and three are we, have mercy on us." That was the only prayer they knew.

"Are you hermits?" the bishop asked.

"We don't know what that means," they replied. "We just came here to praise God by remembering that he is three and we are three."

The bishop was a little worried at this, and he set about teaching them the Lord's Prayer. They worked assiduously, and after a full day, they had finally managed to learn it. The bishop blessed them and got into his boat, admonishing them to remember the prayer.

When the boat was a way out to sea, someone cried, "Look! What is that?"

Skimming the water was a light moving toward them. As it approached, they saw the three old men gliding rapidly on the surface of the waves. Approaching the boat, they called out to the bishop, "Father, we have forgotten your prayer, so we came to learn it again—just tell us from there!"

The bishop crossed himself and said, "It is not for me to teach you. Your own prayer will reach the Lord. Pray for us sinners." He bowed low before the three hermits.

The holy men turned and went back across the sea. As they receded into the distance, their song could still be heard, "Three are thee and three are we, have mercy on us."

God himself is the teacher. Grace works on nature, but we are open to God's direct action as well, capable of knowing him by any means he desires.

There is a moment when God calls you. It is as if he sounds a note, as on a tuning fork, and it reverberates in your heart. It might resound in the midst of a busy Harlem street or in the depth of solitude, on a train or airplane, or on a crowded New York subway. But you hear it unmistakably. "Now!" it says. "Now! Arise and go." Go to this place or that. Go speak to this person or that one. Arise, go, write this book or article. Arise and be reconciled with your neighbor. Arise and take the step for which I have been preparing you.

The last thing you want to do is to arise and go, because when God calls us, he purifies those he chooses through suffering. If you follow him, you could be spit upon or have stones thrown at you. You could be called "white meat," as I was when I spoke about racial justice in the Deep South during the 1940s. But when you hear God's call, it is more agonizing to sit still than to obey. Such was the experience of Jonah, of Jeremiah, and of many other prophets.

There will be a tremendous turmoil in you. You will feel as if you're being ripped apart. This is the beginning of your journey inward, the moment of realization that the Holy Trinity dwells within you, as well as outside of you. It is the moment of prayer. Not of long prayers, not of prayer as you or I might understand it. I don't even mean the Eucharist. There is something else, something simple. The moment you hear God's call is a moment of recognition, receptivity, and deep openness. It is the moment when all we have to do is realize that we are creatures, and it is God who calls us. It is Love who calls us, God our lover. He is calling us to what each of us most deeply desires: a life that will bear fruit.

Sterility is the most tragic thing that can happen to us. Remember the parable of the fig tree? (Luke 13:6–9)

God offers us fertility. He offers us a life of unimaginable fruitfulness, because he offers us the possibility of helping him build his kingdom. What is that kingdom? It is you and me, and the girl who takes drugs, and the alcoholic down the street. His kingdom is the lame and the blind, the lonely and the jobless, the rich and the poor. It includes all races. It is the whole world.

We crave greatness for our lives, and God asks us to become little. To pass through the door that leads to his kingdom, we must go down on our knees. Paradoxically, if we do so, we will find ourselves growing in stature, for "no eye has seen and no ear has heard…all that God has prepared for those who love him" (1 Corinthians 2:9).

This is a moment of choice. One of many, for we will be called to choose every day until we die. We are utterly free to turn back from this power that draws us on. We are free to loose ourselves from the bonds of a love that demands our total surrender. Nothing prevents us from saying no. Nothing except God's love.

Prayer becomes simple: "I believe; help my unbelief!" (Mark 9:24 RSV). He is used to that prayer. Often, it is not even voiced aloud. It is a cry of few words, a cry of agony, a cry for help, a wordless cry for clarity. Behind these short cries, accented with pain or sorrow, or sometimes joy, lies the plea, "Help me to move on, to wherever you want to take me." "Happy are those who have not seen and yet believe" (John 20:29). Faith grows as we journey inward toward the heart of the Trinity.

Sometimes it is difficult to enter into this fire and movement and wind. We become sluggish. We seem not to care. Prayer ceases to mean anything to us. The days become gray and routine. We are tempted to say, "What does it all matter?" This type of suffering is atonement, a plea for forgiveness, even the payment of a debt, if you want to put it that way. Such suffering is not devastating. On the contrary, it liberates us. It is permitted by God so that we might advance up the mountain of faith. It is part of our prayer, part of the journey inward.

Prayer is contact with God. To make that contact, we must smash the idols that we worship within ourselves. Not until we begin the journey inward do we realize how numerous these idols are. We must take a sledge-hammer to ourselves and smash them, one by one, in order to reach the fire and the wind and the movement of the Trinity. We tend to cling to these idols, afraid to recognize their existence in ourselves, and we worship them without fully realizing that we do so. They must be smashed. They are like stones tied to the kite of prayer so that not even the Holy Spirit can lift it.

To free our prayer, we must stop hiding our faces. Next, we must open wide our arms so that we are cruciform. Now, we are revealed to others, exposed to their gaze. The beginning of that self-stripping corresponds to Christ's, whose stripping began when he became incarnate as a child and gradually increased until his human body lay naked on the cross, a sign of his boundless love for us.

What is asked of us is that we go deeply into the hearts of men. We cannot do this unless we are invited. We will not be invited unless we are willing to reveal ourselves to the other, saying, "Yes, I know the hell you're going through. I've been there, too. I can surmise what you're feeling because I've had a similar experience, though perhaps not as deep as yours." Now there is a rapport between us and the other. But to become naked in this way, to bare one's soul, is very, very hard. It's like opening the door to our innermost self, giving to someone the key that leads to the kingdom of God within us. This is a land without frontiers. I hand you the key to my heart and say, "Come in."

Are we ready to open ourselves in this way? Do we want to love God and our fellow man totally, completely, defenselessly, without manipulation or the exercise of our own will, attentive to the tuning fork of God? Are we ready to pray the prayer of a creature called by God to a love affair with him? If we are honest, we must answer, "Lord, I cannot do it without you. Teach me how to grow in faith. Teach me how to love. Teach me how to pray."

God is love, and our religion is a love affair between God and man. Its essence is faith. "I do have faith. Help the little faith I have. Give me more faith so that I might bear the fruits of love, tenderness, peace, justice, and truth, for the world and for myself. Lord, help me to grow in faith, which is the father of all these things."

If the darkness becomes too dark, and the pain and confusion too great, turn to a priest. One of their fundamental roles, besides the celebration of the Eucharist and the other sacraments, is to show us how to grow in faith, hope, and love. Thus they become a shelter for us when the cross grows too heavy. Let us not hesitate to ask this of them, for in doing so, we call them to their true identity.

To me, prayer has always been a matter of listening. All my life, I have desired passionately to listen to God. When I was a little girl, I used to run in the low hills that were covered with wild flowers. My mother would say to me, "Where have you been?"

I would answer, "In the hills."

"What were you doing?" she wanted to know.

"I was listening to God."

"How did you listen to him?"

"Oh, it's very simple," I said. "You just lie down and the wind goes through the wild flowers, and they bend back and forth, and God speaks."

I was little then, and my imagination was vivid. But if you keep listening to God, one day you will see him, and this is what makes it an adventure. Now, I get up in the morning, and I begin to listen as I move through the day. As I do so, a tremendous peace comes upon me. I dictate letters, I sort donations, I look at books, I talk with members of the community and with visitors. Sometimes people are not feeling up to par. There is anger and irritation. The voices become a cacophony that rolls over me like thunder. But I smile and listen, and answers come, because somewhere deep, deep within, I have peace, God's peace. In the midst of the turmoil around me, this inner listening brings peace. On a human level, I might be mad at the things going on, but it is like a storm over an ocean. Fifty fathoms down, everything is calm. Man is like that. The storm can rage, but as long as there is peace beneath it, all is well. It is a way of participating in the sufferings of Christ.

There is a tremendous joy in all this. At a given moment—for an instant—this wind comes swooping down to take you into the inner heart of that fire we've been talking about. It doesn't burn you, doesn't scorch you. It is warm, tender, caressing, and you emerge from that fire cleansed. You forget about your inadequacies and weaknesses, because you know they don't matter to God. He doesn't care if you're not perfect. He simply wants you to come into that fire to love him, to merge your love with his until you yourself become part of that fire, until everything is ignited by its sparks. "I have come to bring fire to the earth," he said, "and how I wish it were blazing already!" (Luke 12:49)

What Am I?

Am I a stone, O God, for you to write upon with fire? If so, O Uncreated One, give me the strength to bear your fire.

Am I plain desert sands upon which once again you burn a bush of fire? If so, O Uncreated One, give me the strength to bear your fire.

Am I a sea or mighty lake upon which you walk again with human feet leaving burning imprints? If so, O Uncreated One, give me the strength to bear your fire.

Am I a tiny square of earth beneath a Cross, consumed and eaten up by drops of your precious Blood falling from your fiery Wounds? If so, O Uncreated One, give me the strength to bear your fire.

Do you desire all this fire you pour into my soul to light and warm someone? If so, tell me who? Or do you wish me to consume myself with love for you alone? Speak, Lord, Beloved, speak. Or else your stone, your sand, your water, and your earth will die beneath the fire of your infinite desire. If so, O Uncreated One, give me the strength to bear your fire.

Prayer and Doing
the Will of God

It is not those who say to me, 'Lord, Lord,'
who will enter the kingdom of heaven, but the person
who does the will of my Father in heaven.

Matthew 7:21

It terrifies me sometimes when I hear young people say, "God told me to do this or that, to go here or there." One girl who was visiting us said to me, "I didn't go to the laundry because the Holy Spirit told me I should take a walk instead."

I have seldom heard God speak to me in this way, at my own bidding, and in accordance with my own needs and desires. Under such circumstances, how can a person say with assurance that he is doing the will of God? It is easy to say, "I received all this in prayer," or "I came by this subconsciously," but unless it is checked by someone else, a neutral person and preferably a priest or someone with knowledge of the spiritual life, such a statement will ring false.

I believe God inspires and draws people here and there, but it makes sense in terms of the circumstances surrounding that person's life. A woman wrote to see if she could come and join us. She was convinced that she had a vocation to the lay apostolate. It turns out that she had a husband and five children. It didn't take much to figure out God's will in that situation.

Today young people want to make pilgrimages. I'm all for pilgrimages. My mother made pilgrimages. She loved them and would readily walk two hundred miles or more to visit a shrine or a holy place. But there was more involved than just the urge to get up and go somewhere. First, the children had to be cared for. Secondly, it had to be a time when my father was away and didn't need her. Thirdly, the household had to be in good order. If one of those conditions were lacking, she would not go. God speaks to us, but what we hear must be checked out in relation to our responsibilities and our particular way of life.

God directs our lives. He directs them through the Ten Commandments, and especially, through his law of love: we are to love him with our whole heart, mind, and soul, and our neighbor as ourselves (Luke 10:27). "By this love you have for one another," he said, "everyone will know that you are my disciples" (John 13:35). He asks us to love our enemies and to lay down our lives for each other. If we do that, we are certainly being directed by God.

The sanctity of St. Therese of Lisieux was such that she obeyed even those who misdirected her. She went to the pope for discernment about her vocation, and only then did she enter Carmel. Then, she found herself under the authority of a superior who was not very pleasant, but she obeyed to the letter. In the convent, her sense of obedience to the rule was so great that when she was writing and the bell rang, she would lift her pen from the paper without even finishing the letter she was forming.

In the 1930s, I wanted to sell all I possessed, go to the poor, and live alone among them in a poustinia in the marketplace. When the idea came to me, I immediately checked it with a priest. I checked it with countless priests. They all discouraged me, saying, "You have a son, and you are both mother and father to him." They told me that what I thought was an inspiration of the Holy Spirit was a temptation from the devil. One priest advised me to sprinkle holy water on my bed at night. I obeyed him. In fact, I drenched the bed so thoroughly that I had to sleep on the floor.

The discernment of these holy priests turned out to be wrong, but in the end, it didn't matter. I did my best to accept what they told me but couldn't get away from the pressure of the Spirit. It became so great that I couldn't stand it. What did I do? My father had said, "If ever you are in a difficult situation, and you don't know which way to turn, go to the bishop. He is the father of your soul." I went to Archbishop Neil McNeil of Toronto; he allowed me to do what I had to do.

In this way, our apostolate has existed from its very conception under the seal of obedience. I have never disobeyed a bishop or the Church. A visiting bishop once said, "I've heard that Catherine has had many difficulties, but there is one thing she stands for unquestionably. She is obedient to the magisterium of the Church." That is absolutely true. I have been accused of every other sin in the book, but no one has ever accused me of disobeying the Church.

I cannot differentiate between prayer and obedience. How can I pray to God, who was obedient unto death, if I myself act contrary to obedience? Christ my brother came to do the will of my Father, and I must do likewise. I must do so through pain, rejection, and misunderstanding. Today God is raising up many people who honestly and sincerely desire to pray. But how can God listen if a person prays to do his own will? I cannot judge another, but on this point I stand before the Almighty in fear and trembling. As close as I feel to God, these are moments when I know he is terrible and awesome, and I prostrate myself before him, knowing I am nothing.

We tend to pray with great intensity for things we want, but do we think of praying for what God wants? Usually, when our desire for something cools off, so does our prayer. It is important, therefore, that when we pray, we move with the current of God's will, and not against it. This is true even when we are praying for someone we love tremendously.

When my husband, Eddie, was in a car accident and I was on my way to be with him, I prayed fervently that he might be well. But in my mind, every second, I forced myself to add, "If it be thy will." If God wanted to take Eddie home, for whatever reason, I had to be willing to accept it. I was ready to do God's will and to move in its stream.

The greatest act of a Christian is to do the will of God. How do I know his will? How do I know which ideas are mine and which belong to God? To know his will, I must learn how to listen to him. This can happen only through prayer and under the guidance of a spiritual director.

Try to think of listening as an essential part of prayer. You pray, and you hear the voice of God speaking to you gently, not out loud, but deep in your heart. If you listen carefully, you will begin to know his will for you. God wants us to do his will, and he gives himself to us continually, that we might follow in his footsteps.

Because you are in love with God, you can relate to him as you would relate to a boyfriend or girlfriend. You can talk to him in order to find out what he thinks. You want to do as he suggests. Listen to him then, that you may know. God speaks quietly, very quietly, but he does speak, and he will make known to you what he wants you to do.

You will do his will, and it will be beautiful. To do what God wants you to do is to be truly happy. Sometimes his will may bring pain, but it will also bring you joy. Everything comes from God, and everything returns to him in our hearts. To give ourselves wholly to God, in prayer and in action, is the life of a Christian, and in it we discover joy so immense that our ordinary, everyday life is completely transformed. We find ourselves living in a new reality.

Listen, that you might hear and understand what it is that God wants of you. Listen to him quietly and follow him. You will be filled with joy. You will also be filled with pain, but that makes no difference, for "your sorrow will turn to joy" (John 16:20).

If We Surrender

How strange your ways, Oh Lord. On the brink of despair, you make love. If we surrender to the duty of the moment, we shall discover great joy and beauty in it.

My Father's House

"Anyone who does not welcome the kingdom of God
like a little child will never enter it."
Then he put his arms around them, laid his hands on them
and gave them his blessing.

Mark 10:15,16

Many believe that everything has to be sifted through the mind, and once that is done, they turn to God, saying, "Okay, Lord, I've looked this matter over, and this is what I've decided to do." Unbelievable as it seems, we ask God to comply with our decision. We dare to believe that our intellect might even occasionally match his. But there is another reason for our behavior. Deep down, we are afraid that if we leave it to him, we will be crucified. And we are right.

Never forget that you can do nothing on your own. The essence of any vocation is prayer. We pray in order to know the will of God and accomplish it, for Jesus said, "Cut off from me you can do nothing" (John 15:5). What, then, is prayer?

The prayer above all others is the Mass. We worship God in the sacrifice of the Holy Eucharist and render glory to him. Communing with him, we commune with the whole world. Unless we communicate with God, we can do nothing, but when we receive God, we communicate with man. This is the foundation of our lives as Christians.

At the moment of baptism, the Father, Son, and Holy Spirit come into the soul. The Trinity dwells within me. I can touch God. Even as a baby, I begin my first steps toward union with him. Some might say, "Some are called to perfection and others are not. Trappists are, secular priests are not. Nuns are, lay people are not." The truth is that the whole world is called to a state of perfection through living the gospel. Everyone, by virtue of baptism, is a contemplative, because everyone carries the Trinity in his or her soul.

Prayer is love. Imagine a dance. There might be fifty people on the dance floor, but suddenly you pick out one girl in the crowd, and her eyes meet yours. From that moment on, no one else exists for either of you. The girl goes home and can't stop thinking of every word you said to her. "What a guy! He told me my eyes are bluer than all the rivers in the world." What's she doing? She is meditating on the words of the man with whom she has fallen in love.

Meditation is as simple as that. You don't have to sit before God, hemming and hawing, wondering what on earth to say to him. Be natural. One of our Madonna House priests tells us not to worry about meditating when we come to chapel in the morning. "All you have to do is be there," he says. "If you feel like sleeping, go ahead. That's not a bad meditation—it's like going to your Father's house and stretching out on your brother's bed, because you're close to him and you know he won't mind. Your brother is Christ."

I remember once in Chicago when I wanted to say the Stations of the Cross. It was a hot day in the slums. When I got to church, I lay down on one of the benches and fell asleep like a baby. Two hours later, the sacristan came around and said, "Hey, lady, this is no place to sleep."

Still groggy, I answered, "Of course it is. It's my Father's house."

I'm not suggesting that you sleep in churches. The point is that prayer is simple and natural. God is someone you fall in love with, and you respond to him accordingly. Like the girl at the dance, you hang on every word that he says. You listen with your ears, with your mind, with your heart, and what he has to say sends you soaring. If you had been one of Christ's apostles, wouldn't you have stayed awake at night pondering things he had said that day? You would have treasured every word. Meditation is thinking about everything my beloved friend has said.

One afternoon, I was in Central Park in New York City watching a boy and girl sitting, their hands clasped, gazing deeply into each other's eyes while a little mongrel dog devoured their picnic lunch unnoticed. They never saw him, and they certainly didn't see me watching them. They weren't even talking. They had reached the stage of love where silence said all that was necessary. True lovers contemplate each other wordlessly, and so it is between us and God.

Prayer is constant. When I was taking a refresher course in nursing at the Montreal General Hospital, one girl who worked with me, Georgina, used to sing as she carried the bedpans around the ward. "Look, Georgina," I said, "you're going to get in a lot of trouble if you do that. You're supposed to be discreet when you carry bedpans, not parade them around singing like you do."

"Who cares?" she answered blithely. "I'm in love!" And off she went.

It was a surgical ward, and the men applauded her. She was an excellent nurse and her love never interfered with her work, but obviously it filled her thoughts all day long. That's what love is like, and that's what prayer should be like.

If you believe that Christ is your brother, then, little by little, you will come to know him. As your heart grows purer and more childlike, you will come to see his face more and more clearly. My favorite prayer is, "Lord, give me the heart of a child, and the awesome courage to live it out as an adult." Your prayer will be continuous, never heavy or difficult. Your love will be always before your eyes, and your prayer will be within you. God is your Father. Christ is your Brother.

You Who Are Crucified

You, who are crucified, you know that day and night, I dream and fight to take you off the cross of hard, cold, human hearts. Tell me, you, my Beloved, who hang so high and yet so low against a fearsome sky aglow, and drink the bitter, bitter draught of mankind's old and endless pride, while at its feet you let your precious blood seep, seep, to be trampled by its clay feet; tell me, Beloved, how can I change these stony hearts?

You see, if you helped me, I could become a fire of desire that would melt stone. For you have come and walked with us and worked and played. Perhaps you sang. But then, why should you sing? Each word you said contained all music. You came, you lived in our midst, you preached, you died of love, and you allowed the holy women to walk with you. So now, if only you will tell me how, I too can make my soul a veil. Nay, not my soul alone, all of myself, and show your love and, thus, perhaps take you off the crucifix of men's proud and dead hearts.

Ah, my Beloved, there must be a way to take you off that crucifix of death that men continue endlessly to crucify you on—their dead and hard hearts. Make me a chisel, that I may break the crucifix of human hearts, or drill them into tiny stones that will become soft, loving sand. For you know, Beloved, that day and night I fight to take you off the cross of hard, cold, human hearts, and in so doing, make them a loving inn where you can rest.

Answering Youth's Hunger

May he give you the power through his Spirit
for your hidden self to grow strong,
so that Christ may live in your hearts through faith.

Ephesians 3:16

There is a great sadness but also an immense joy in me these days.

When I look around and see youth turning their faces toward God in meditation, prayer, and fasting, I rejoice. Around us in Combermere, some of the former so-called "hippies" or "flower children" came to settle on the land. They were among the most earnest of their generation, and it is amazing to see how dedicated they are to their ideals. They have survived the first winters, rugged ones with temperatures falling to -20 and -30° F. They chop their own wood, fix up flimsy old farmhouses to make them weatherproof, and bake their own bread. Even more exciting, however, they fast and pray. These two arms of prayer and fasting have been lifted to God throughout the centuries, and the young people of today continue to do so.

Some of them talk of meditation and contemplation, of Zen Buddhism and karma, Confucianism, Taoism, and other Eastern religions. This is the cause of my sadness. I say to myself, "What is the matter with us Christians? For us, prayer should be like breathing. We have known meditation and contemplation since Old Testament times.

Why are we not answering the cry of the young by teaching them these fundamental ways of reaching God?"

One of my favorite descriptions of prayer comes from the book, *The Struggle with God*, by Paul Evdokimov:

> "Pray without ceasing," insists St. Paul, for prayer is at the same time the source and the most intimate form of our life. "When thou prayest, go into thy room, and closing the door, pray to thy Father in secret." This means to enter into yourself and make a sanctuary there; the secret place is the human heart. The life of prayer, its intensity, its depth, and its rhythm are a measure of our spiritual health and reveal ourselves to us.
>
> "Rising long before daybreak, [Jesus] went out and departed into a desert place, and there he prayed." With the ascetics, "the desert" is interiorized and signifies the concentration of a recollected and silent spirit. At this level, where man knows how to be silent, true prayer is found; here he is mysteriously visited. (p. 176)

"Here he is mysteriously visited." We are taught to pray by Christ, and the Our Father is the prayer he gave us. But when we are standing still and very silent, he visits us in yet another way. He comes to us himself, and the scriptures are opened to our understanding as if cracked by a nutcracker, the nutcracker of the Holy Spirit. The meaning of the words is released, and we are filled with joy and knowledge and awe. It is Christ himself who is teaching us.

Evdokimov continues:

[I]f one does not know how to give a place in his life to recollection and silence, it is impossible for him to arrive at a higher degree and to be able to pray in public places.... The water that quenches thirst is distilled in the silence that offers us the indispensable withdrawal to view ourselves in the right perspective.

Recollection opens our soul to heaven, but also to other men.... St. Seraphim says, "Acquire interior peace and a multitude of men will find their salvation near you."...

In this present time of verbal inflation that only aggravates loneliness, only the man of prayerful peace can still speak to others, and show them the word become a face and a look become a presence. His silence will speak where no preaching can reach; his mystery will make others attentive to a revelation that has now become close and accessible to them. Even when he who knows silence speaks, he easily finds the unsullied freshness of every word. His answer to questions of life and death comes as the amen to his perpetual prayer....

The essence of the state of prayer is to hear the voice of another, that of Christ, but likewise that of the person I meet, in whom Christ addresses me. His voice comes to me in every human voice; his face is multiple: it is that of the wayfarer to Emmaus, of Mary Magdalene's gardener, of my next door neighbor. God became incarnate so that man might contemplate his face through every face. Perfect prayer seeks the presence of Christ and recognizes it in every human being. The unique image of Christ is the icon, but they are innumerable, and this means that every human face is also the icon of Christ. A prayerful attitude discovers it. (p. 177–178)

Prayer is such a simple thing. It has its own rhythm. You get in touch with God, and then you get in touch with yourself. Before I can love my neighbor, I have to love myself. Then I can love everyone else.

There is a sort of intangible rhythm of prayer. Man stands before God with his head bowed. His hands come together in a gesture of greeting, a gesture of prayer. He is embarking on that journey inward that every man must take if he is to meet the Triune God—Father, Son, and Holy Spirit—who dwells in him. Having bowed the upper part of his body, man stands up again. Stretching out his arms, he discovers that he is cruciform. The tips of his fingers can now touch people, because he has touched God.

This rhythmic movement of prayer is an important way of using one's body. Throughout the day, pray with the totality of yourself on the inner journey, penetrating deeper and deeper into the silence and solitude of your inner being. Contact with God and one's fellow man takes place on an ever deeper plane, for God is love, and our relationship is a love affair between God and man. Making contact with God inevitably must lead to making contact with man. In other words, prayer is for the service of man.

In the process, *kenosis* takes place. *Kenosis* is the Greek word for emptying oneself in order that Christ might grow in us. What does that mean? It means that the dimensions of our heart must constantly increase. Because Christ became incarnate in humanity, we too can take humanity into our hearts. We can serve humanity in a thousand ways, including fasting and prayer.

Fasting and prayer can never be for oneself. They are always for the other. Modern youth, but not only the youth, are seeking ways and means of emptying themselves of the self-centeredness and greed that permeate our North American culture. They want to empty themselves so that God might fill them, and so that "through him, with him, and in him," they might be of service to their fellow man. Why are we not giving them the answers? Why are we not preaching the glad news of Christ himself, so that people might recognize in us the features of the God we claim to worship and believe in? Why do they have to turn to non-Christian religions to find food for their souls and lives?

Some years ago, the bishop asked me to attend a theological conference in Toronto. One day, I was wandering around in the sunshine when I came across a group of hippies sitting on the grass at Toronto University where the conference was being held. They had just been evicted from their residence or something, and people were bringing them sandwiches.

One girl spotted my cross and asked, "Are you a nun without a religious habit?"

"No," I said in my blunt way, "I'm a person."

That must have been the right answer, because before I knew it, she was calling to her friends, "Hey! She's a person! Sit down," she told me. So I did.

"Do you know J.C.?" she demanded. (J.C. is Jesus Christ.)

"Baby," I said, "do I know J.C.? I know J.C. like no one knows J.C. Compared to you, I'm like an astronaut passing a milk train!"

That impressed her. "What kind of trip are you on?" she wanted to know. "L.S.D.? Speed? Grass?"

"Nothing like that. I'm high on Jesus Christ."

She couldn't believe her ears. "No drugs?"

"No nothing," I said firmly.

Then we talked. We talked and talked. I spent ten days with her. I told her all about St. Teresa of Avila and St. John of the Cross and other great mystics of the Catholic Church.

"Gee whiz," she kept saying, "they're better than Zen Buddhism!" Needless to say, I agreed.

That was one of the most amazing things that has happened to me. It was beautiful. The kids wanted me to be their guru. "What about the generation gap?" I asked. They assured me that with gurus, it makes no difference.

Those were the years when the hippies started coming to Madonna House. They were searching. They were hungry for God. They fell in love with Our Lady. Many of them gave up drugs.

If that kind of thing could happen to me, at my age, just imagine what could happen with younger people, solid in their faith, going out to reflect the face of Christ and preach the gospel with their lives. It is time we stopped discussing peripheral issues and plunged into the abyss of faith. It is time, and the time is now.

What Have You to Offer Me?

And what have you to offer me,
In whose blood flows wild anarchy?
Are you the Sun with potent fire

To infiltrate my slow desire?
Are you the wind to sweep my blood
Gratuitously to such a flood?

Finding Christ
in My Brother and Sister

Grace and truth have come through Jesus Christ.

John 1:17

I have a question. I have many questions. What Catholic these days doesn't have a questioning heart and mind? All my questions converge into one fundamental point: How can I find Christ in my brother and sister if I first do not know Christ personally?

Like many in Madonna House, I read a lot. I read current books and a number of periodicals from several viewpoints—liberal, conservative, left-wing, underground, and so on. I see a trend emerging. With the revival of some degree of social consciousness, with the dawning realization of the state of minority peoples throughout the world and of the need for interracial justice, and with the growing recognition of the inequality that exists between rich and poor countries, Catholics and other Christians are realizing that we must seek Christ in our brothers and sisters.

Some people, though, feel that the personal approach to Christ through the sacraments and so-called "old fashioned" ways of prayer is obsolete. Their emphasis seems to be more and more on social justice, the elimination of poverty, the improvement of interpersonal relationships. More and more, I hear and read that the best way to encounter Christ is in and through another human being.

How can I find Christ in my brother and sister if I first do not know Christ personally? I could not recognize him in my brother had I not first met him personally.

What do I mean by this personal meeting? I mean the very essence of our faith. Christ gave us two commandments: to love God and to love our neighbor, in that order (Matthew 22:38–39). To love someone, I must know him. To know him, I must meet him. It is only when I meet and know him that I will recognize him in others.

How do I get to know Christ, so that I can love him and continue to love him in my brothers and sisters, and love them because I love him? Christ knew me first. He knew me when I was baptized into his death and resurrection (Romans 6:3,4). Now he dwells in me. I know him when I undertake the journey inward into my own heart. I know him in the "breaking of the bread" (Luke 24:30,31). I know him when he kisses me with "the kisses of his mouth" (Song of Songs 1:2), when I kneel at his feet in confession in repentance and sorrow. I know him through the Holy Spirit who came to me at confirmation and who abides with me always.

I know him in prayer of all kinds. I know him especially in the great prayer of silence, the inner silence of my own heart. Breaking his own silence, he speaks when my heart ceases to be noisy, and I beg, "Speak, Lord, your servant is listening" (1 Samuel 3:9).

I can learn much about God through books and techniques of the mind, but there's a vast difference between knowing about God and knowing God. Only those to whom he reveals himself know him.

This brings us back to prayer and the sacraments. In the sacraments, we make contact with God the Father, God the Son, and God the Holy Spirit. Through the sacraments, we come to know God directly, tangibly. Then and only then can we go forth to all humanity. Only then can we recognize his face in our brother and sister.

To me, this is the essence. Many of the ideas I read are on the periphery, like moths darting hither, thither, and yon around a light. How can we love our brothers and sisters if we do not love God first? Love of man is the fruit of our love for God. If the love of God is not there, why bother calling ourselves "Christians"? We are mere humanitarians.

Seeking

I seek thee, Lord, so long, so passionately, without ceasing, but your mysteries close in on me, for there is nothing easier than finding thee. You are "they," my neighbor, everyone whom my eyes touch. You are bread, wine, served to me these days on platter golden at Mass. But your mysteries close in on me. My eyes are held, beholding neighbor and strangers passing by. Bread and wine on golden platter plunge me into faith darker than the darkest night. Yes, your mysteries close in on me. Yet I go on, for I am driven by love that knows no end, to come to your dwelling amongst us children of men. Yet again, dark faith engulfs me, lifting me to unknown heights or dashing me into immeasurable depths.

I seek thee, Lord, so long, so passionately without ceasing. Yet all I have found is darkness, depths, heights. These have led me to more hunger for you, Beloved. Behold me then, a pilgrim of love appearing before your hidden face, my Lord, wrapped in your mysteries with nothing but faith and loving hunger to pierce them with.

Without Me,
You Can Do Nothing

Remain in my love.

John 15:9

"I am the light of the world" (John 9:5), said Christ. Since he has come, we are no longer living in the shadow of death. We can live in light.

But without darkness, we would not know the light. God allows us to enter the darkness because he intensely desires that we identify with him who took on himself the darkness of sin. In the darkness, we experience our helplessness and powerlessness. In the darkness, we are blind. Now, God can heal us. The act of faith takes place in darkness, where intellect cannot penetrate.

When we enter this darkness of faith the light eventually bursts in, but not right away. First, God says, "If you believe in me, come. Walk on the water." The apostles were dumbfounded when they saw Jesus coming toward them on the water. Peter started toward him but began to sink because he lost faith (Matthew 14:22–33). Most of us are too filled with fear to even start out. St. John said, "Perfect love casts out fear" (1 John 4:18 RSV). We are so fearful that we cannot even imagine that kind of love.

There is a story of a child in a burning house. His father is outside calling to him, "Jump! Jump!"

"Daddy," the child cries, "I can't see you!"

"That's okay," the father says, "I can see you."

In our technological age, we want to see where we are jumping. We want to see not only the father whose arms are stretched out to catch us but the earth beneath our feet. We want everything sorted out and in order. We are afraid to walk into what seems chaos to us. It is really perfect order, but we cannot see that. We want to say to God, "Let's get organized." God refuses to organize himself to our standards. We cannot manipulate him—but oh, how we try!

Meanwhile, the world cries out in agony. It cries out for salvation. Humanity may not know to whom it is praying, or whence help will come, but still it cries out. Jesus is the one who saves, and Christians are called to love mankind and to assuage its pain. How can they help? How can they bring so many millions to true life? How can they bring justice and mercy to a twisted, needy world? Only by the power of God. Christ has said, "Cut off from me you can do nothing" (John 15:5), but if we are one with him in prayer, we can do everything.

The answer to our modern problems, whatever they may be, is to turn toward God with lifted hands, moved by love, trusting in God's promises and mercy. There is no other answer. If one stands in intercession with uplifted hands, as Moses did, then the miracle of God's action will take place (Exodus 17:11).

It seems strange, but the prostration of prayer, the dance of prayer, the rock-stillness of prayer, or whatever form prayer may take, floods the whole world with action. He who turns his face to God in prayer is in the eye of the hurricane, the eye of action. Somehow, the miracle takes place. Man remains on the mountain before God (Exodus 32:11–14); at the same time, by the power of his prayer, it is as if he walks the earth with his towel and his water (John 13:1–5). Prayer changes things.

When we pray, we have accepted Christ's invitation. Not only did he say, "Cut off from me you can do nothing," but he went on to add, "If you remain in me and my words remain in you, you may ask what you will and you shall get it" (John 15:5,7).

We must lead each other to the top of the mountain to pray, because prayer is dynamic and holy. It is contact with God and union with him. As a man grows in union with God, he comes to know that prayer includes all righteousness and from prayer stems all the goodness that God wants to bestow on mankind.

Prayer is a person moved by his whole being to communicate with the living God, to respond to God's love. Prayer is this response that takes a thousand postures, from standing with arms uplifted in supplication to full prostration. Prayer is the movement of a dancer, and prayer is the stone-like stillness of a person utterly immobile, lost in regions that few enter. Prayer is the bubbling brook of a child or quivering words from the lips of old people. Prayer is the words of men, women, and children who know God and easily talk to him. These words change into beautiful songs when they reach God.

People recite the rosary. They pray for all their relatives and all the needs of the world, vocally, simply, in a childlike way. Even when they sleep, their hearts watch for the Lord. When they pray, when they worship God, they are caught up in something greater than themselves, something cosmic. The whole universe bows in adoration to God, and those who love him join in that adoration.

God is the only way. He is the only answer. And the only way to lead men to God is to teach them prayer and to pray for them.

Black Fire

The quiet hush of your presence filled me. But I was held in a dark misery, with bands that tightened around my heart, in the cold, dead, blackness as of night. And I was gouged by a black fire that seared and burned without heat, without light, but its penetrating light of knowledge disclosed to me the ugliness of sin. And knowing your beauty and infinite perfection, I was filled with loathing steeped in a weight of love pressing against the bands around my heart.

O helpless Love, to see you hurt, to see you bear with infinite patience and such forgiving tenderness the careless thoughtlessness, the cold ingratitude, the noisome weight of sin, of my sins. I had asked to bear your burden with you. Was this your way of showing me the weight of your cross, the pressure of the crown of thorns around your head? Only the knowledge that you could see my misery, that you could know the limit of my strength, that you could ease the burden of your love upon my heart, sustained me.

Prayer as Eating
the Word of God

He who eats my flesh and drinks my blood
lives in me and I live in him.

John 6:56

The Mass is the greatest of all the love songs. It is our daily rendezvous with God, where he comes to us joyfully and gladly.

The imagery of the Song of Songs and of the many scripture passages where God is spoken of as bridegroom or spouse brings us to the essence of prayer. Meditation, contemplation, songs of prayer lead to the union of man with God, not only in the hereafter but now. And what has begun through other kinds of prayer is brought to fulfillment at Mass. God and man become one in a strange and incredible mystery that only a lover as God could conceive. The Mass is the incarnation of his immense love and the incarnation of our response: God and man are in communion. Perhaps at this moment, prayer as we understand it ceases, and the mystery of being possessed by God is revealed: you experience the Mass and it totally encompasses you.

I am especially joyful when I go to Communion, cognizant of the mystery happening there. For me, the symbols of bread and wine dissolve and disappear into the reality of Christ's body and blood. I receive God in a mysterious way. The Mass has a tremendous power to unite me with him and all of humanity. He comes to me in order to be united with me. When I receive from the chalice, it is difficult for me to let go of it. The symbolism has vanished and only the blood of Christ remains. I want to hold on to it as long as I can.

One day at Mass, the idea came to me that we eat the Word of God. As I waited in a state of anticipation for Communion, I suddenly said to myself, "Catherine! Every day you feed yourself with the Word! The Word can be eaten!"

In the scriptures, an angel tells the prophet Ezekiel to eat the scroll on which were written the words he was to speak (Ezekiel 3:1–3). This isn't exactly the kind of experience I'm describing. It isn't so much that you swallow the Word but that the Word penetrates you and fills you. You read the Word of God at Mass, but it is more than reading. The Word absorbs you.

The Word of God is related to unity in a way so deep it cannot be expressed. It is related to *sobornost*[3], the Russian concept of total unanimity of heart, mind, and soul that takes place in the Spirit. It's as if the footsteps that Adam and Eve heard in the twilight move toward me, and I am absorbed by God, absorbed by the Word. We read in the scriptures, "In the beginning was the Word." All that God the Father created, he created through the Word (John 1:1–3). It staggered my imagination to think that the Word could become one with me in this way and I with him. I could actually eat the Word and become totally permeated by it. It becomes part of me. Depending on how completely I absorb it, I reflect it visibly, its rays emanating from me. I eat the Word with unequaled love

---

3. See *Sobornost: Experiencing Unity of Mind, Heart and Soul* by Catherine Doherty, Madonna House Publications, 2000

and passion. The Word fills me to overflowing. You see its reflection in me.

I become one with the Word I eat. I cease to exist. The Word absorbs me because I am willing, because I say to God, "Let me dissolve before my death. Let me be filled with you, so that every step I take is your step and every gesture I make is your gesture." This is beyond abandonment, beyond kenosis, beyond anything I can describe. It is like the void where one meets God. I have surrendered to the Word. I have eaten it. I am filled. The Word preaches through me.

From early childhood, I have been imbued with the scriptures, and throughout my years in Madonna House, I have had a sense of this process going on within me. The more I absorbed him in the scriptures, the more he absorbed me. Finally, one day at Mass, I was able to say, "Okay. I cease to exist. Now you are everything."

I'm still human, and I'm still living right on this earth. But I eat the Word of God, and this gives me the strength to live and preach the scriptures. Most of my old fears and terrors have left me. I can say, "I live now not with my own life but with the life of Christ who lives in me" (Galatians 2:20), for I eat the Word every day.

We are all afraid, filled with feelings of doubt and rejection. I wish we could simply cry out to God, "Lord, you kiss me with the kiss of your mouth through the Eucharist and through the Word. I eat your bread and drink your wine. You are the greatest physician, and I come to you directly, you who can heal us so quickly."

We can throw ourselves onto God. He is like an immense sea. He is like a cape that envelops you. He is a friend when everyone seems to have abandoned you. "Look, I am here," he says. "Give me your hand." Now you realize that you have never really been rejected. Your emotions no longer churn and cloud your love for those who have hurt you. You love because God loved you first (1 John 4:19).

The sea is warm and waiting. Listen to the waves calling you: "Come. I'll make you whole. Come. My waters will make you whole."

A Lover

Mighty, infinite, uncreated, why do you love us dwellers of earth? Why do I, insignificant earthling, feel the compelling, ecstatic whirlwind of your love? Why do I know without knowing that I am alone in a crowd; that for you, crowds are all separated into brides and souls, and that for each one, you would die your thousand deaths in a few hours on a Friday afternoon? All that is human in me dissolves at the thought. Like molten lava, it flows on itself and consumes all that it touches, which is myself. Then again, your breath, the wind of your love, touches the lava, and I am myself, a woman, an earthling again. And again, the thought of your loving me, apart from the crowd, lifts me into heights that reduces me to nothing again. And again, a touch of your breath resurrects, and your love makes me whole again.

How can I exist in this knowing that is an unknowing? How can I remain unconsumed while I am being consumed—a lover?

Prayer of the Towel and Water

He had always loved those who were his in the world,
but now he showed how perfect his love was...
and began to wash the disciple's feet and to wipe them
with the towel he was wearing.

John 13:1,5

God writes straight with crooked lines. I remember the passage from scripture that says, "My thoughts are not your thoughts, my ways not your ways" (Isaiah 55:8). What appears hopeless to man may be exceedingly hopeful to God. On my last lecture tour, I walked into what seemed an explosion of hope.

We in the developed countries have sinned. Lost in our affluent society, we have given generously from our surplus but scantily from our necessity. Several years ago, potatoes were being burned in the U.S. Northwest, because they couldn't be sold. In the Canadian West, grain was allowed to rot. This could have been given to those who need it. Because we have sinned against our brother, we have sinned against ourselves. What will we find, we who have hated our Black brother, disliked our Indian brother, and often despised anyone different from ourselves?

We have sinned in not fulfilling Christ's second commandment, which tells us to love our neighbor as ourselves. We haven't loved ourselves and, thus, we haven't been capable of loving our neighbor. We present-day Christians have sinned by not showing the face of Christ to the world at large. The early Christians showed his face to such an extent that the pagans said of them, "See how they love one another."

Why, then, do I feel hopeful? I feel hopeful because the Lord has plowed a field, harrowed and seeded it. I feel hopeful because green shoots of prayer are rising from hearts everywhere, not only from those dedicated to religious life but also from men and women of all vocations. People are praying in their hearts and taking time to go to quiet places to reflect. They are being drawn inwardly toward him who poured himself out in the service of others.

I see quiet service rendered by one person to another in great simplicity. It isn't frantic, where people rush to the ghettos to become social workers or leave their ministries to become psychologists and what have you. It is a quiet service, person to person. That is what Christ desired. His life was spent in prayer and service, and so must our lives be. We must not only love our neighbor; we must take the time to listen to him, to have a personal relationship with him. This is possible for everyone, wherever you live. In high-rise apartment buildings, private homes, and condominiums, you can reach out to your neighbors.

You seek community? The greatest and most fundamental community is the Trinity who dwells in your heart from the day of your baptism. I touch the Trinity within me. I extend one hand toward God and the other toward my brother. This is community. If I don't reach out toward mankind, the hand outstretched toward the Trinity will fall limp, because God will not grasp it. God and man, man and God. I am now cruciform.

In his inimitable way, God brings forth this prayer from the hearts of all. In this prayer of love and service, all arrogance, enmity, desire to manipulate must disappear. Unless we love each other as Christ loved us, we can pray and read scripture all we want, but nothing will happen. At the core of our prayer, there must be love.

Strive for hospitality of the heart. Without it, hospitality of the house is nothing. We must accept those who come to us just as they are, without judging them and with deep respect. The traditional Russian Christians greet their neighbor, "My brother is my life, and my brother is my joy." When you meet your brother, do not probe and do not ask questions. If you stand there like Christ, accepting the person as he is and taking him into your heart, God will reveal what he wants you to know about that person.

This attitude of always and everywhere opening one's heart to the other requires spiritual warfare. We must fight against all that is not God within us. This is *kenosis*, the emptying of oneself in order to be filled with God. This is true poverty. When you touch God, you serve man, and you are crucified. What can you hold on to? Nothing. Not even your will. That is poverty. The things of God are simple—we are complex.

When I am cruciform, I am free. I am holding on to nothing. I can be a carrier of the towel and water, wiping the feet of my brother. This is the answer to all of our social and political problems. My forgiveness and love of you, and your forgiveness and love of me—until this takes place, expect nothing to happen.

O Lonely Christ of Charing Cross

O lonely Christ of Charing Cross, Rue de la Paix, Boulevard Anspach, O lonely Christ of a thousand celebrated thoroughfares and foreign-sounding streets. Why is it that I have to meet you here, so far from home, when I have seen you lonely too in Harlem and Fifth Avenue? In Edmonton; Yukon; and Portland, Oregon; Chicago, San Francisco, Kalamazoo, you were lonely, too.

O lonely Christ of everywhere, why stand you there and here, so still, so sad, looking at the hurrying crowds pass you by—why? Why are your eyes so full of hunger, longing, pity, and compassion? Why do you lift your nail-torn hand, and then let it fall again with so much sadness, as though you were a beggar about to beg, alas? Why is it that I have to meet you across all continents, all celebrated thoroughfares, strange, dingy streets and palatial avenues, as well as wild and distant places?

You answer nothing. You just look.

O Christ of Charing Cross, so lonely, you weep because the multitudes are hungry for your love and know it not. And because you hunger to be loved by these who know you not.

Give me the key, Beloved, so that I may open your loneliness and entering, share its weight. Behold my heart that you have wounded with love. Make it a door for all to come to you. Give me your voice and words of fire that I may show them *you*.

The Duty of the Moment

I live now not with my own life
but with the life of Christ who lives in me.

Galatians 2:20

We are so busy these days. It's as if we are on a merry-go-round or roller coaster. Faster, faster, faster—that's us. We don't know if we're going forward, backward or which way. So here we are, living in a world that goes on all around us—more selfish, more greedy, more horrible than before. Faster, faster, faster it goes. But Christ said that he came to serve (Matthew 20:28), and so should we. Christ said to pray at all times (Luke 21:36). So we should. But how? How do we live in this world today? How do we serve? The answer that I've seen, after 50 years of this lay apostolate, is to do the "duty of the moment."

The duty of the moment is what you should be doing at any given time, in whatever place God has put you. If you have a child, your duty of the moment may be to change a dirty diaper. So you do it. But you don't just change that diaper, you change it to the best of your ability, with great love for both God and the child. You can see Christ in that child.

Your duty of the moment may be to scrub your floors. If you see to it that your house is well-swept, food is on the table, and there is peace during meals, then a slow order is established, and the immense tranquility of God's order falls upon you and your family, all of you together.

The essence of our vocation is to connect ordinary and seemingly boring life with Love who is God. We must do the will of our Father as Christ did. We must give our whole self to it. We have to do the duty of the moment with our whole person: mind, heart, soul, body, emotions. Thinking about or getting emotionally involved in some need outside our duty of the moment can make us fragmented, not totally given to the present moment. "The revelation of the present moment is an ever freshly springing source of sanctity.... The present moment is the manifestation of God" (Jean-Pierre de Caussade).

Our vocation is hidden, yet this is the place God has called us to—the place where he will enter our heart and strip it naked of all that is not his in order to dress it in the bridal garments. "Everything is a means and an instrument of holiness; everything without any exception. The 'one thing necessary' is always to be found in the present moment. The 'one thing necessary' is what each moment produces. What happens at each moment bears the imprint of the will of God. Treat it as a sacrament which hallows by its own power" (de Caussade).

Doing the duty of the moment, living the nitty-gritty, daily routine of ordinary life can uncover the face of Christ in the marketplace. Christ can come into the place where you work or play or eat. He will come into your home or into a restaurant. He will come into a school or a company cafeteria or a subway or wherever. Doing routine duties of the moment with enthusiasm and joy: the floor shines brighter, the windows are cleaner. Not only them—you shine, resembling closer and closer the icon of Christ. Your eyes reflect God.

When I first came to North America, I had to support my sick husband and our baby, so I had a job as a waitress and that was my duty of the moment. I was working at a restaurant near Wall Street in New York City and every day a fat gentleman would come in and eat pies. He would eat loads of pies. Half pies. So, one day, quietly, I said to him, "You must love God very much, dear sir."

He looked at me rather strangely. He said, "What do you mean?"

I said, "Well, you're eating so much of this pie, it will get you back to him fast—before you know it."

He looked at me and said, "What you're trying to tell me is that I'm committing suicide through my fork."

I said, "Well, I wasn't going to put it that bluntly."

I was about three inches away from him, and he looked at me and said, "Lady, you've got something there." And he gave me a five-dollar tip.

The next day he came in and said, "Okay, what do I eat?"

I said, "A salad."

So, you see, there is a way to be a waitress and there is a way to be a waitress. He said, "You show very much concern, not only to me, but to that gentleman over there, too. He's so thin and you're always feeding him more."

I said, "Well, I hope you do not object to my bringing religion into this situation. I believe in God and I believe that God said, 'Love your neighbor as yourself.' So you're fat; I want to make you thin. He is thin; I want to make him fat. That, I think, is loving each other."

He said, "Gee whiz. I must tell that to my wife."

I didn't preach. I didn't say I was Catholic or Protestant. I just said, "You're welcome."

So this is what I mean. You, as a Christian, as a follower of Christ, do your duty of the moment. Whatever your duty is, you do it with great love. And as you do, the image of Christ, the icon of Christ, will be shown to people wherever you are—in your home, in your place of work outside the home, in your school, in the neighbor-hood where you live, in your church, in the grocery store, wherever you happen to be.

It's fine to say, "Praise the Lord," and so forth, but re-member that Christ said, "It is not those who say to me, 'Lord, Lord,' who will enter the kingdom of heaven, but the person who does the will of my Father in heaven" (Matthew 7:21). What's the will of the Father? It's so sim-ple. It's the duty of the moment.

There are plenty of good things you can go out and do, programs and such, but whatever they are, you have to realize that there is always the duty of the moment to be done. And it must be done, because the duty of the moment is the duty of God. Tired, un-tired, sick, well, whatever your state, do the duty of the moment. It's what God calls us to do. And if we do it, people follow us. We don't have to preach by word of mouth. We preach by living. We preach by doing. We preach by being.

I feel that God calls me to atone. How? Doing the duty of the moment can be an effective atonement for tragedies, for sins of the nations. Just do as he tells you. Live your life for everybody, and start with the duty of the moment. How do you show the face of Christ to a world that is secular, atheistic, indifferent, greedy, and selfish? By do-ing what he asks you to do. And his voice is very simple. He says love God with your whole life, your whole heart, and love your neighbor as yourself (Matthew 22:38–39).

Resting peacefully on God's breast, listening to his heartbeats, we find the answer to our question: "What must I do?" God simply answers, "Do what I ask you to do. The duty of the moment is my duty. And I want you to follow in my footsteps, no matter where they lead. Do not use your normal intelligence to evaluate my footsteps. Just walk in them. Be simple, be childlike." At first this is perhaps a rather loud yes or *fiat*, but as years go by, it becomes almost a whispered one. I train myself to listen to God and to pick up or drop, do or stop, pray or work.

When you do the duty of the moment, you do something for Christ. You make a home for him in the place where your family dwells. You feed him when you feed your family. You wash his clothes when you do their laundry. You help him in a hundred ways as a parent. Then, when the time comes and you appear before Christ to be judged, he will say to you, "I was hungry and you gave me food. I was thirsty and you gave me drink. I was sick and you looked after me" (Matthew 25:35–36).

I am grateful, especially in the darkest moments, for the duty of the moment. It is one of the greatest gifts of God to mankind, that he set us out a series of duties to do throughout the day. The duty of the moment is like a sturdy walking stick one takes on a long hike. It's solid, and in the darkness on the trail it's like a third eye. Open yourself to his will so that, day after day, nothing matters but his will. You say, "Lord, here I am. Speak. Your servant listens," and, "Lord, send me wherever you wish." We find this totality of surrender to the will of God moment by moment, day by day. It means being able to endure personal difficulties because we see Christ in each other. Love makes every gesture, step, word, and work, redemptive.

Christ in Me

Beloved, you speak to me through people, things, and events. You send your messenger, the duty of the moment.

Touch my eyes, my ears, my will. O Jesus, help me to see clearly and to recognize the first principle of active work—union with you. All my exterior actions must reflect your life in my soul. All duties of the moment are the path to you, Beloved. I am coming to you in the duties of the moment.

I must prepare my soul for you, Beloved. I must adorn it with meekness, humility, detachment, poverty of spirit, mortification, unselfishness, charity. I pledge myself, again and again, daily, to work only for love of you and for your glory. Help me. Increase my love for you, for in it alone will I find strength.

Do Little Things
Exceedingly Well

Let everything you do be done in love.

1 Corinthians 16:14

Madonna House is the place of little things done well for love of God. It is a lay apostolate, very, very ordinary. By doing little things with love, you radiate; you contribute to restoring the world to Christ. Co-redemption is love and an acceptance of a daily gray routine without glamour. An ordinary life lived in an extraordinary way.

Any place you go, you will have little things to do. But there seems to be a lack of connection between little things and daily life lifted up into the heart of Christ. The daily routine of a believer whose heart contacts God's heart is no different from an unbeliever's. He or she gets up in the morning, has some chores to do, goes to work, cares for the children. Little things become big when they are touched by God; when you are a light, when you are adventuresome, joyous, glad, simple, humble, direct.

Little things cannot be separated from love. How can you give in to the feeling of monotony when you're in love? When you do dishwashing with the attitude that it's a beautiful little thing you can give God, it becomes an adventure. It all hinges on this personal God, this sense of adventure, on the sense of call. You have to make connections between every gesture you make, every breath you take. Little things become a cascade of precious gems, of gold, of grains of incense, if we open ourselves to be loved by God and to love him back.

Little things include kindness and thoughtfulness. Picking up after yourself and others so as not to burden your brother. Not lingering in the bathroom. With great love, answering the same questions repeatedly. Returning tools to their places. Being punctual. Leaving the kitchen tidy.

Today there is lots of sloppiness in the world: in making your bed, in clothing yourself. Little things are apt to slip into the background. Little things at first appear to be irrelevant and matter-of-fact. Yet, little things are the very essence of sanctity and spiritual formation.

We take no pride in the work of our hands; in fact we sometimes despise it. It appears to be a lack of humility, the heresy that menial work of any kind is degrading. The attitude seems to be that if you have an academic degree, menial work should not be assigned to you. So deeply ingrained is this heresy in youth, men, and women that I am at a loss how to tackle it. But the heresy persists among us and breaks the bond of charity, creating confusion and chaos at times. All the great contemplative orders, as well as the mendicant ones have in their constitutions time allotted to manual labor. Every founder and foundress understood clearly the dignity of manual labor. Christ was a carpenter, a manual laborer. This didn't just happen to him at random. He chose it. Our Lord showed that he came to serve when he washed the feet of the apostles (John 13:2–16).

Little things are thoughtfulness, reverence for things. Gather up the fragments let they be lost: a look, a word— opportunities for grace to come to another person, let me be attentive to all and not miss opportunities to see and do little things. That one farther step, that one true smile that comes from the depth of your heart and not only from you lips.

We begin our vocation full of joy, with high resolutions and glowing hopes. Then we chafe under the monotony. It's natural to look for the exciting, the emotional, the satisfying in life, but it's better to look for what God is teaching me in the place where I go or where I am. Boredom means a person has let his inner resources become comatose, that his motivation (his love of God and man) is at absolute low ebb. Boredom spells grave danger. How can we be bored when we have the marvelous words of St. Paul telling us, "It makes me happy to suffer for you, as I am suffering now, and in my own body to do what I can to make up all that has still to be undergone by Christ for the sake of his body, the Church." (Colossians 1:24)! It is in his mercy that God calls us, through grace, to become co-redeemers with him. God has given us this immense power—which is worked out through our daily routine: typing, cleaning, driving, fixing things. It's a great mystery that our humble efforts to serve should be lifted up by God to bring souls to him.

Think of your vocation, your state in life, as the glory of the cross; think of little things in contrast to what he has done for us. I must lie on the cross Christ gives me, and not the one I make for myself. The duty of the moment demands a total surrender of one's will. Defying peer pressure and being ostracized for it. To be ridiculed, calumniated, persecuted. "The sufferer in his own time finds himself a great distance from former concepts when he felt that he had to offer God and the world something grand, something beautiful, something illustrious, something 'worthy.' He knows now that the great secret is simply not to withhold anything, not even wretchedness, if that is all he has" (John Howard Griffin). What is God's idea of greatness? Simplicity, humility, meekness, forgiveness. What matters most is a willingness to be used, rather than an inner conviction that we have something to offer.

The answer to our pain is prayer. Nothing else will do it, nothing else. With prayer it becomes a joy. Everything is small in relationship to God. The only thing big about you is your hunger to love, to be and do for God.

God asks us to become little. It takes a long time to see reality through God's eyes, the reality of the sanctity possible in ordinariness. Madonna House was built on humility, simplicity, ordinariness, merging with the poor, reflecting the icon of the Christ of the poor. All these little things are the fingers of God the Father shaping you into his Son.

I often think of Christ as a beggar, begging for our love. Before my eyes is a crucifix. To me, it is living, breathing, full of wounds, and Christ is saying to me, "I love you. I love you." Against that crucifix, my whole life is nothing, a tiny little thing. It is the essence of our vocation to connect ordinary things with Love—who is God, to connect little things with restoring the world to Christ.

The Path to Love

I love you, and my hourly prayer is to love you more. Help me, O Jesus. Detach me from the spirit of the world—the blame and the praise. Let me walk the path of life hidden in your Sacred Heart, doing all this for love of you and for no other reason. How full my soul is of determination and desire to serve you and you alone in love. But look at my weakness. Take pity on your child and walk with me, for without you I am as nothing.

Prayer of the Heart

He told them a parable about the need
to pray continually and never lose heart.

Luke 18:1,7

When you are in love, only one person matters to you, the beloved. Others are just a crowd of people. When our beloved is God, we must recognize that he is the king. We must surrender to him. The self has to disappear. Prayer is this self-emptying. It means that we stand still and wait.

Kyrie Eleison, two Greek words meaning, "Lord, have mercy." "Lord, have mercy on me." The picture of a child being born in a cave comes to my mind, a child who is God Almighty. The Father so loved us that he sent his only son to save us (John 3:16). "Lord have mercy." I fall prostrate before this Father. Lord, I cannot believe in that kind of love. Have mercy on me. Enlighten my intellect. *Kyrie Eleison. Kyrie Eleison. Kyrie Eleison.*

As I skip along the road of life, I stumble and fall flat on my face. Perhaps my folks are sick. Maybe I'm not feeling too hot myself. I can't find the words to pray. So, from the depths of my being, I cry out, *"Kyrie Eleison! Kyrie Eleison!* Lord, have mercy on me!" I am no longer asking for intellectual enlightenment. I am crying out for help.

"Our Father, who art in heaven...your kingdom come, your will be done" (Matthew 6:9–10). We say that often but are we committed to his will? Are we willing that it be done in us? In the Old Testament, God constantly thunders against his Jewish people, calling them to look after their poor and their hungry, their orphans and widows. He is furious when a rich man grabs the last acre of land belonging to a poor person. Ceaselessly, he inveighs against injustice of every kind. He told the Jews they were proud, that they were haughty, that they refused to listen to his word. He sent them prophet after prophet, just as he does with us. Today, as at the time of Christ, God says, "In so far as you did this to one of the least of these brothers of mine, you did it to me" (Matthew 25:40). Do we hear him? The poor are still with us, and we do not treat our brother as Christ.

We can sense when our actions do not conform to our prayer. We know in our heart that our life is not an icon of Christ, not even a smudged icon. "You will be able to tell them by their fruits," said the Lord (Matthew 7:20). Prayer is like a tree: when the fruits are bitter or nonexistent, something is wrong with our prayer. "Lord, have mercy." Here is the source of our greatest joy. When we acknowledge our situation, our sinfulness, we can say with joy, "*Kyrie Eleison.*" The moment I say that and mean it, I am forgiven. Again and again, I am forgiven. With God, every moment is the moment of beginning again.

In the continuous act of love that flows from God to man and man to God, there's one accent that must be incarnated in prayer: rendering glory to God. The person in love with God knows who he is and who God is. He knows he is a creature, and he glorifies God out of the abundance of love in his heart. He can't help it. He must incarnate this in daily life or be untrue to himself.

This glorification of God is like a chant, a song bursting forth from the heart of man. Out of the fullness of love comes song. Songs of love, of pain, of joy, of sorrow.

These prayers are the Psalms that we use for the liturgical hours of prayer—vespers, matins, lauds. They're vocal prayers but still must be prayed from the heart. We pray from the heart when we are in love.

To pray, we need few words. The Our Father is the perfect prayer—Christ himself gave it to us. But suppose you really pray the Our Father. You say those two words, "Our Father," and a whole world opens before you. What does that mean, "Our Father"? When you say, "Our Father," you are immediately taken into the depths of the Trinity. Other associations follow. The Prodigal Son comes to mind. It may take you an hour or two to get through these two words.

"Who art in heaven." You push your mind heavenwards. But where is heaven? "In me," you answer, for the Lord said in so many words, "My Father and I and the Holy Spirit will come and dwell in you" (John 14:9–26). Heaven is in each one of us. When I die, I will explode! I will be in heaven, and I will know the One who has always been with me from the moment of my baptism. All the way to heaven is heaven, for Christ is heaven. The kingdom begins in this world.

We are *anawim* before God. An *anawim* is a nobody, the poor man of the Lord, the poor man of the beatitudes. He knows he is nobody and doesn't preen himself. He doesn't strut about. He knows he is a creature. When he looks at his creator, he knows and adores him. He prostrates before his Lord. The *anawim* is a nobody and, at the same time, a friend of God, the brother of Jesus, and the temple of the Holy Spirit. He is covered with the mantle of the Mother of God and helped by all the saints. He is a creature, but what a fantastic creature! He can count on God. It is almost as if God will come down at a snap of the fingers, for he said, "Whatever you ask for in my name I will do" and "Whoever believes in me will perform the same works as I do myself...even greater works" (John 14:12, 13).

We must understand that these two faces of man are one. We know that we are nothing. We realize that we are weak. Now we can allow God to manifest himself. This is what St. Paul was speaking of when he wrote, "When I am weak, then I am strong." This is why the prayer of the publican was, "God, be merciful to me a sinner" (Luke 18:13). He stood at the back of the synagogue and said it over and over. In this prayer, we find all that we need to say to God. None of us is righteous enough to stand before him face to face. If I think only of his judgment, I despair. But I can count always on the infinite mercy of God.

The Jesus prayer might be enough for us: "Lord Jesus Christ, Son of the Living God, have mercy on me, a sinner." Why would it be enough? Because it brings Jesus into your life. The repetition of the holy name brings the presence of the person. In the Hebrew tradition, the name of a person is the person. We read in the New Testament that all beings "should bend the knee at the name at the name of Jesus" (Philippians 2:10). When I invoke the name of Jesus, I myself cease to exist. I am drawn into his name, immersed in his name, immersed in him.

Even in our secular society, a name is something very powerful. When I say the name "Boris," for instance, I immediately think of my first husband. A person, a lifestyle, a whole period of my life becomes present. Certain names evoke particular events in our lives.

Some names suggest tremendous beauty, others evoke fear. Say the name of Adolph Hitler, and everyone shrinks, even the younger generation that barely knows about him.

Say the name of Stalin, and you have a similar reaction. But when you say the name of Jesus, "it is accompanied by its immediate manifestation, for the name is a form of his presence," says Paul Evdokimov. Just say "Jesus," and whoosh, God is here. You brought him. I brought him. Before the name of Jesus, every knee must bend. When you say "Jesus," many things begin to happen.

That is why cursing is so dangerous for the one who curses. Fortunately, most people in English-speaking countries have learned about Jesus at their mother's knee, and when they swear, they don't really mean what they say. When that name is really used as a curse, however, the curse falls on the head of him who utters it.

When you say "Jesus," the word is already a prayer. You remind yourself, "For where two or three meet in my name, I shall be there with them" (Matthew 18:20). How much truer this is when we say, "Come, Lord Jesus," as we do in Advent. "Come, Lord Jesus." And he comes! This is reality, one of those strange mysteries that exist between God and man. Man calls, and God abases himself and takes again the form of a servant.

Once you begin to pray the Jesus prayer and understand what you're doing, it will continue without you consciously willing it. Once you've called on the name of Jesus, his name will remain with you because you desire it to be there. He desires it to be there, too. The two desires merge into one.

Don't try too hard to concentrate. I might be reciting the Jesus prayer as I talk to you, even though my mind is on a hat I saw a few days ago. I can continue saying the Jesus prayer with a hat on my mind. You don't have to get all upset, saying, "That hat! I wish it would go away. It's been interrupting my thinking and my prayer for days." You needn't worry about things like that.

Russian Christians didn't practice yoga, mantras, special breathing and all the prayers of the non-Christian East. Nor did the Greek monks; they prayed the Jesus prayer naturally, and the Russians learned it from them. "Lord Jesus Christ, Son of the Living God, have mercy on me. Lord Jesus Christ, Son of the Living God, have mercy on me." In and out. In and out. You don't do it consciously; it just happens. This is the Jesus prayer.

Lost in Your Immensity

Lord, I am lost in your immensity. I cannot find its frontiers. There is nothing to guide me anywhere, except, of course, you.

I am not lost as men would use the word, but I am lost in your immensity. I did not know your heart was so immense. I did not know it had no frontiers at all. Stupid of me, I know, for you embrace earth, spheres, constellations; all things that are beyond the ken of men are playthings for you. I can see you playing with the stars just for the fun of it. Yes, I do. But as for me, I am lost. I try to tell haltingly, as little children talk, how you brought me to your void—yes, your void.

I thought and said that there one rests in peace. But I did not know that in your void, which is no void at all but an intensity of fire and of prayer—I did not know that the void was you, and that you brought me there to pray in me, so that I ceased to be, and you possessed me utterly, completely, and you prayed in me. So that is the void I talked about so innocently, so ignorantly.

Yes, I am lost, Lord. I am lost in the void of your love, and I am lost in your heart whose frontiers are beyond my ken or any human eye or mind or thought. Yes, I am lost, but now I know at least one thing. I know that when I enter your void, I cease to be. They call it "all senses suspended"—at least the old writers do. But it's not true, not quite true, because the senses are not suspended, they are alerted, they are filled to the brim with you.

Why do you bring me into the void, your void? Slowly, like a child learning to walk, I begin to understand, for in my hands outstretched toward you, you place your Church. I did not know she was so heavy. I did not know she was so wounded. I did not know she was so torn—just like you. I did not know she, too, was flagellated by men into morsels. That's another face of your Bride: the face of infinite pain, as if the pain of all the world were gathered in your heart. Yet, so it must have been, for she is your Bride, and the pain of all the world is always in your heart.

True, you died for the pain, for the sin that causes the pain most of the time; you died for all of it, to bring us back to Abba, your Father and mine. But as your Father said about his chosen people, we are stiff-necked, and so we did not listen. Perhaps we didn't hear at all, but most of us went about our business of silver and gold; and so the Church was flagellated, too, even as you.

All this immense void you handed me. But who am I? You know only too well that I am a nonentity, a refugee, one who does not belong anywhere, and in a sense, perhaps, belongs everywhere, but not in a way that I can always feel. For I am human, God, and so I feel just like you did when you were human.

I am lost, Lord. Holding my hands forward, carrying the Church, I don't know where to go, what to do. I am in your void, Lord. Guide me, or I shall perish under the weight of your Bride.

The Great Pool of Silence

More than all else, keep watch over your heart,
since here are the wellsprings of life.

Proverbs 4:23

Prayer begins when one turns his face toward God. It could happen in childhood or at any point in life, when a person realizes who God is and what prayer is. When it happens, the scriptures become a million love letters from God to be savored, meditated upon, absorbed almost to the point where you become one with those eternal, fiery, gentle words. Reading scripture is like a conversation with God, a conversation that never stops, because every sentence moves the heart to greater love.

Praying the scriptures brings silence to our minds and hearts. Words in themselves can be terribly confusing unless one reads the word of God slowly and consistently. When you read the scriptures in this way, they penetrate your being. You may not be able to quote chapter and verse, but the thoughts enter your heart. They become filled with light. You read the words and say, "Oh! That's exactly it! This is God's way of talking."

I myself have the childlike belief that God really does speak to me in this way. When he speaks to me directly, it can be rather frightening and awesome, but when he speaks through the scriptures, it often seems less so. Suppose you are thinking about something and are frightened. Opening the scriptures, you read that God said to the Jews, "Come now, let us talk this over" (Isaiah

1:18). This is precisely what we are doing with him when we read his word. Do you remember how God rebuked the Jewish people before he said this to them? He has reason to rebuke us too, but he invites us to sit down and talk, and suddenly things are different. When we realize we are speaking to God, our use of words changes.

Words are pregnant, pregnant with meaning. They may be pregnant with good or pregnant with evil. They may be filled with God, the devil, or simply with ourselves. We must pay attention. When our words are filled with self, we are vulnerable to the devil, for we cannot be filled with thoughts of the self and others at one and the same time.

God, of course, is the Other, and all "others" blend into him. When I pray, he stands before me. I cannot get away from him. I leave all that I have to follow him. He became man to take upon himself all other human beings, with their sins, their sorrows, and their joys, because he loved us. In God, I meet my brother, who is my life.

Words are pregnant with meaning, and I think it is for this reason that the Church calls some of her sons and daughters to a life of silent prayer. In this holy silence, we learn discernment. In the great silence that takes hold of men and women as they grow more and more familiar with the written word and with the Word Made Flesh, all words find their true meaning.

In my book, *Poustinia*, I shared some of my thoughts on the silence of the heart. I want to speak more about this. A pure heart is a silent heart. A pure heart watches carefully over its words. This doesn't mean that one cannot speak. The silence is the silence of love. My heart is silent, and thus an inner space is created where I weigh my words. The words that come at me from without also enter that silence and are evaluated there, not in accordance with my emotions but my love. All sorts of hurtful words that make me feel rejected and abandoned or whatever it may be can be thrown into this great pool of silence. The silence of love, coming from a pure heart, will examine with wisdom all that is said to me, and this love will determine my response.

It is like a laundry. The words thrown at me go through the cleansing process of love, faith, silence, and hope. At this moment, what we call "discernment" becomes crystal clear. God himself reveals the meaning to me. Why didn't he do this before? Because he wanted the words to pass through me first. He wanted me to accept the unjust things said, because this acceptance is my identification with him and part of my own divinization.

Christ died to make me divine; thus, I am a co-heir with him. To claim this inheritance, I must experience what he himself went through. Whenever impatience, complexity, or emotionalism take hold of me, twisting and turning the truth as often happens when the devil gets his hand in things, then I can descend into the pool of silence where I think it over, pray about it, and purify my heart and thoughts. This is the laundry of the Spirit, the purgatory of the Spirit here on earth. When I enter this pool of silence, I become more charitable. Is there any limit to charity? The only limit is death. I die for the other out of love for him. This was the only limit that Christ himself knew.

In the pool of silence, I learn to be open. Openness is a door that never closes, a door that has been taken off its hinges. The gaping place where the door once stood now announces, "Friend, come in. Here God is spoken about with love." Our hearts must be open to all hearts. It is important to learn this in the pool of silence, because once you open that door, you cannot close it again. You will be hurt, and you will have to face and accept that hurt. It is easier to accept being hurt by strangers. I expect the Communist to hurt me, but I don't expect to be hurt by my friends. Great pain can come. People will walk through that open door of your heart, and they will hurt you. You must be ready as Christ was ready. He was hurt physically, mentally, and psychologically. At one point he thought that even his Father had abandoned him. He died for us. If he was ready for this, so must we be.

When we are prepared for pain in this way, something strange happens to us: pain results in joy. If I am prepared for the possibility that the person who comes through the open door of my heart may hit me, and if I believe I belong to God, this is a moment of joy. When you are ready for pain, it not only hurts you less but also has an influence on the other. You may not see its fruits, but they will be present. We must accept the fact that pain is inevitable for the follower of Christ.

The only ideas for which we are permitted to fight are in matters of conscience. Otherwise, our ideas must be plunged into the pool of silence. I don't know what happens there. Whatever it is, once your thoughts are plunged into that vast pool, you begin thinking before you speak—but you don't think with your head. You think with your heart, and everything changes.

Do we want to open our hearts? Do we want to open them to pain, to joy, to everything? Our motive must be charity, because that is God's motive. If that is our motivation, and if we truly open our hearts, then we will automatically think alike in matters of the Spirit. Sobornost, oneness in the Spirit, will be ours.

You have opened your heart, I have opened mine, and we have gone together into the pool of silence where God is present. We begin to use words carefully, almost haltingly, and our words become different. As our words change, the doors of our hearts open even wider. As they open, people enter. We begin to know each other, and we become one in the great pool of silence.

A Soul's Question

Into the strange, awesome glory of your face, you drew my soul. In that immense, immeasurable power, I am a nothing that reflects your light. The weight of the light would bring me death. But you pour into it your life. O Lord of hosts, of might and glory, O uncreated, infinite One! What traffic have you with dust? Do you rejoice in seeing a speck of dust dance in your light? Or, incredibly, does your mercy deign to fill this speck of dust with your own life? Into the strange, awesome glory of your face, you drew my soul.

When You Go to the Poustinia

Be still and know that I am God.

Psalm 46:10

Many people all over the world have read my book, Poustinia, but there is so much misunderstanding as to what the poustinia really is that I wilt a little when I think about it.

First and foremost, when you go to the poustinia, don't worry about prayer. Take one book with you: the scriptures. Don't get anxious, saying, "I've got to pray, I've got to pray. How do I do it? What do the scriptures say to do?" No. Walk in, bless yourself, bow to the crucifix or icon or whatever you have, and say, "Peace be to this house and to me." That's all you have to do.

If you're tired, sleep. Have a good sleep, and you'll feel better afterwards. You may sleep for twenty-four hours, but you will be praying while you do so: "I sleep, but my heart is awake" (Song of Songs 5:2). Perhaps you take a walk. It doesn't matter whether you're in the country or the city. Be completely natural. Prayer is rest. Breathe in the breath of the Spirit. Be free. Be simple. Prayer is a perfectly natural relationship between God who loved you first and you who try to love him back.

The other day I received a letter from a woman who wrote, "I went into the poustinia, and I could barely wait for it to end because my head was whirring so." She said she couldn't pray because her head was buzzing with a multitude of concerns and activities. This woman had a false concept of prayer.

The soul's entry into the poustinia is an entry into total relaxation. Maybe you're too neurotic to relax at first. In that case, let the poustinia itself relax you. There's nothing to get excited about. Unless you settle down and find peace in the poustinia, you'll never be able to reach the union with God that you seek there.

If you want a cup of coffee or tea, go right ahead. Drink 20 cups if you want. Divide your bread into three sections for breakfast, lunch, and dinner, or if you prefer, eat it all at once. There has to be a sense of freedom and simplicity about these things. In the poustinia, there's absolutely no structure. When people go to the poustinia, their first question is "What do I do?" What would you do in a real desert, alone with no one to talk to and only the scriptures at hand? Do that in the poustinia and be free about it. Be utterly, completely free. Be free from anything that would distract you. You're outside the normal restrictions of time and can do what you please.

You have come to the poustinia to pray. What does that mean? Of course, it's good to pray for everyone, but the Lord knows himself what everyone needs. Leave your lists of petitions outside, and say to him simply, "Lord, you know I come with all the needs of all the people who want me to pray for them, but I am simply going to give them to you and let you take care of them all." That ends the conversation.

You're going to meditate. What's that all about? It's as if you had a boyfriend or girlfriend and you sit thinking nice things about him or her. In other words, you think about the person you're interested in. The person who really interests you is God. So you think about him.

You think about his words, which you can read in the scriptures,

But there is something else. There is contemplation. "Contemplation" means to look at someone in silence, and this is where the poustinia comes in. You enter the poustinia in the silence of a heart that has ceased to worry about anything and is completely open to the other.

Whether you are looking at the trees as you walk, looking at the people on the city streets, or just sitting in your little room, the face of Christ is before you and your face is before him. You are lost in the heart of him who loves you and whom you love. That is all. That is the poustinia.

A bride instinctively throws herself into the arms of her bridegroom. She doesn't say to herself when he comes home, "Now, what am I going to do? Shall I throw myself into his left arm or his right arm?" When you go to God in the poustinia, just put your head in your heart and really see him. Be simple, be like a child, and have fun with God. There are no structures, and no one can tell you to do this or that.

Do not confuse the poustinia with a prayer house. In the poustinia, one person lives apart from everyone else. It may be a room in a house with others, but when you enter the poustinia, you are alone.

Another unusual aspect of the poustinia is that you don't go to Mass during that time. The Mass comes to you, in the sense that God comes to you in a very special way. You enter into this contemplation, and the poustinia brings you to silence, the silence of the desert, the immense silence where your heart meets the heart of God.

You continue in this silence until you reach the Absolute. It might take a long time or it might not, but in the process, you will become a prayer. You are not praying with your lips, nor with your head. You are not even praying with your heart. As St. John of the Cross wrote in one of his poems, "On a dark night, kindled in love with yearnings…I went forth without anyone knowing, my house being now at rest…to the place where he (well I knew who!) awaited me" ("Dark Night"). In this state, all senses are suspended. When that happens to you, you will have become a prayer, and eventually you will reach the Absolute. This is the essence of the poustinia.

To go to the poustinia is simply to rest one's head on the breast of God, listening to his heartbeats. It is impossible to grasp this with the mind. You will understand it only with your heart—a heart that is in touch with the heart of God.

Let My Heart Repose

O Lord of peace, keep me within your heart. Let me rest upon your breast, no matter where I am. My feet may fly upon a thousand tasks for you, my hands be busy with things to do for you, my mind immersed in thoughts and plans for you. But let my heart repose within your heart, for then I will be truly blessed by you.

I hunger so for that repose in you. My heart is restless unless it rests in you. As time flies by, my heart hungers more and more for silence, for solitude. I am so parched for both; it is like walking in a burning desert to be without them.

Oh, grant me the grace of silence, solitude of heart amidst the milling, noisy throngs who fill my days. Oh, grant me repose and rest within your heart amidst ceaseless activity on your behalf. O Lover, come, take possession of my heart, and keep it forever within your Sacred Heart.

Prayer and Solitude

"Lord, teach us to pray."

Luke 11:1

Prayer is "in." So is solitude. People are talking about prayer houses. They want to run away to a prayer house, hermitage, or poustinia. They want to go live somewhere far away from everything and pray. Are they running from an intolerable situation, that of modern urban living? Or is this just another way of escaping from what irks us? If the latter is true, we will soon discover that what bothers us ultimately is ourselves—the one thing we can't leave behind when we go into solitude. On the other hand, could it be that the voice of God is truly calling this or that person to a certain kind of prayer? How do I know if it is my will or the will of the Father?

Many prayer houses have been born but died in infancy. Some have started but are barely able to keep going. Others ended tragically in quarrels and difficulties. Why? I don't know. I do know that a prayer house or a hermitage without love and peace is not a place of prayer.

Why is there this wave of prayer houses? You might say, "Just look at the evil all around." But my next question would be, "If I am a Christian, should I run from evil or should I enter the ring and fight it?" The real question is: How should I fight evil? By living in a poustinia? By living in a ghetto? By staying in the city? By remaining right where I am?

Our prayer must be upheld by our life. I can spend my whole day praying. I can be a mystic of the first order. I might even levitate or have the stigmata. But the test is always, "By their fruits you shall know them" (Matthew 7:20). Prayer can change things only if I change with my prayer. Then prayer will and must bear fruit, fruit which is acceptable to God.

It is wrong to speak of prayer houses and poustinias as if this were the only way to pray. First, you must make a house of prayer in your own heart. Stand still. Find God in yourself, on your journey inward. Interiorize your poustinia, your house of prayer, in order to find out if God is really calling you to a life of solitude.

It is important to differentiate between prayer and solitude. Prayer is the fundamental act of the Christian, his very life. Prayer is continuous in a heart that loves, and doesn't need solitude any more than a toothache needs solitude, or any more than joy needs solitude. When you are in love with someone and you get engaged, you want to be alone with your fiancé, but you still have to keep on working.

You can make love everywhere, because lovemaking is not only performing the marriage act in bed. Lovemaking can be two people holding hands in a special way. Lovemaking can be two people not even touching each other, but deeply aware of one another's presence.

Prayer is contact with God such as lovers have, such as friends have. It doesn't need solitude to exist. Occasionally, it is nice to have it, but let's not make the mistake of thinking that we can only pray to God if we can get away from the mob and escape to the solitude of a Russian-style poustinia. We have to be realistic about prayer. Prayer is first and foremost standing still before

God. Before you even begin to ask questions about prayer, you must stand still.

How can anyone tell you about prayer? Only God can explain it. You can read about it in a book such as this. You can ask someone who is prayerful, and he will tell you something about it. But the essence of prayer cannot be communicated. None of us can be an expert on prayer. St. Teresa of Avila wrote her books under obedience to her spiritual director, but there are no words to express those kinds of experiences. When you read her books and those of St. John of the Cross, and all the great mystics, you kind of get left behind. Speaking for myself, I read them and then I say, "Well, this is beautiful—but what about me?"

No one can teach us to pray except God. How can I tell you what happened to me and my husband on our wedding night? What has been said and done remains our secret. When our lover is God, prayer is a secret between the King and the one he has chosen for his bride. Prayer is something like a continuous wedding night. It is stillness. It is lovemaking. Who can describe how God makes love to man and how man makes love to God? Who can tell you how man stands still before the miracle of love? Who can describe how you cry out with joy because Christ is a man who runs with us, plays with us, befriends us, drinks a cup of coffee with us? You have to remain still and wait. God himself will come and tell you about it.

Once all this has been interiorized over a long period of time, then perhaps God will call you to solitude. Solitude is a special vocation. It is God saying, "Come with me into the desert and pray all day and all night. I want you to be in solitude so that you might walk among men in the dark of their night with quiet feet."

If solitude is not your vocation, and you have confused it with prayer, you may go off to be alone and then find that you can't pray at all, that the fruits do not justify your staying there. Be careful when you become disenchanted with solitude that you do not leave behind prayer as well.

There is a special loneliness that is part of the vocation to solitude, but loneliness is also part of the ordinary Christian vocation simply because loneliness is part of silence. In order to really pray you need that strange silence to surround your prayer and allow it to come forth. This silence is not an outward reality but an inner one, and this is what all of us have so much difficulty understanding. I don't need solitude to pray, but I do need inner silence. Then I can pray any time. I can even pray as I talk to you.

It helps to have an environment that generates peace. This has always been the Benedictine ideal. But that environment does not have to be a monastery. It can be a family or community that is in love with God, and that therefore creates an environment where people can find the inner silence they need. Whether it be a blood family, a parish community, a university group, or whatever, the important thing is that the members love one another. The important thing is that they love their enemies (parents, superiors, "the establishment"). When we love, the criticisms we make will not be vindictive. If we fail to love, we will be out of touch with Christ, and our prayer life will be fruitless indeed.

Loneliness

What strange mystery is this, O Christ? The closer I approach your love, the lonelier I become. It seems as if, indeed, it is *terribilis* to fall into the hands of the living God. Alone, the shadow of your face crushes my heart and brings about a host of fears. Your weight is so immense; the world seems weightless against your weight. And loneliness complete seems to embrace me, severing all ties with men, yet not binding me to you. Tremendous Lover, is this your way to bring a soul into your courts, where she can wash herself in tears and be bedecked in the heavy mantle of loneliness beyond any known on earth, so that she understands that loneliness is fire of desire for you, the Desired One?

The Land of Loneliness

God, you are my God, I am seeking you,
my soul is thirsting for you, my flesh is longing for you,
a land parched, weary and waterless.

Psalm 63:1

Where does the life of prayer lead? Toward the end of
the journey inward, after one has met Christ and shared
his Cross, one enters a strange land of loneliness. Peace
seems to precede it. I think it is the peace that comes
through having been crucified. There is a moment of
resurrection, as if one has been taken off the cross. The
wounds are not healed, but they no longer hurt.

You are different. You are different because now you
know that God exists, and he alone matters. It is an over-
whelming, awesome thought. It could be an annihilating
thought had you not in some way shared in his crucifixion yourself. You are different in the sense that now
all people belong to you and are part of you, and you
belong to all people. At the same time, you belong only
to God, and you belong to him totally. There is a distinction between you and others, and at the same time, there
is no distinction at all, but a blending of all into one. The
demarcation that exists is a spiritual one, born of what
you have lived and what you can never explain. This is
the land of loneliness.

There are no words for this. The land of loneliness is
the land of joy. It is the land of union with God. The land
of loneliness is the land of hunger for God. The land of

loneliness is one of belonging to God and understanding that God alone matters.

The secret of this land is that the hunger for God grows in you like fire. In fact, it is fire. At the same time, the love of humanity is intensified. There is only one thought in the land of loneliness, one dream, one passion, one desire: to lead people to God.

But people do not want to go to God. This is the loneliness that Christ experienced throughout his whole life, most intensely in the garden of Gethsemane. In the land of loneliness, one knows, perhaps only a little but with intense passion, who God is. You desire with a passionate desire to give him to every man, woman, and child.

Then you discover that people do not want to accept him. They will give him a token of themselves, a part of themselves, but they do not want to give all of themselves to God. So you walk in the land of loneliness. In that land, there is no possibility of manipulating others. You can't do it because God will not allow it. God is in charge, not you. The person who walks in the land of loneliness is on the way to saying, "It is no longer I who live, but Christ who lives in me" (Galatians 2:20 RSV). Not that we aren't still sinners, not that the weight of God doesn't continue to lay heavily upon us, but the call remains to lead all people to God.

To enter the land of loneliness, all my needs must be directed toward God alone. Many of the needs are still there; they have not disappeared. They constitute my tunic, the only tunic worn by the pilgrim in the land of loneliness. Sometimes the tunic seems like a hair shirt; at other times, it is soft and downy. It symbolizes something I have come to understand a little: the fact that we tend to need each other differently from the way in which God wants us to need each other. One of the fruits of this strange journey is that those who enter the land of loneliness are received back by Christ, and they receive everyone back in him.

The need for approval, the need to say everything in our mind, the need to be needed, the need to direct others toward myself, to impress them by my intellect, my capabilities—these needs all fall away. In the land of loneliness, friendship becomes simple and joyous. Because all needs are centered in Christ, my own insignificance no longer matters to me. The one flaming desire to bring all men to God seems to soften the impact of all these things. The human heart, as far is it is able, now opens itself to total possession by God. One understands, in the light of this incredible reality, that without him we can do nothing.

You are reduced at first to a state of seeming non-being. The wings of the intellect fold, the heart opens, and the intellect is illuminated by Christ. Now one understands a little more fully the words of St. Teresa of Avila that "I and a ducat are nothing, but I, a ducat, and God, are everything." To paraphrase her statement: I cannot lead anyone anywhere by myself, but if I allow myself to be filled with God, I can lead men to God.

The road that began at baptism and continued with the Eucharist, confirmation, and contemplation of the Beloved has finally led me through the passion and the cross, and brought me to the land of loneliness. It is a land of strange peace and intense joy, but it is a land of loneliness. I think it is the last step before total union with God. For some of us, many perhaps, this union may come before our death—if we love enough, if our heart is open enough, and if God desires it so.

A Seed

I was a seed of wheat, you were the sower. You buried me into the deep, dark furrow one day so long ago. I died a thousand deaths within that earth so dark, so rich, so warm, so cold, and yet I lived. Twice I believed that it was time to bring forth fruit. But twice the storms of hatred, of scorn, froze the furrow and the earth. Then, when it seemed to me that I died my thousandth death, the rain, the sun came. And beneath its warm rays I brought forth my seeds and laid them in your hands to die again and multiply. Amen.

I put my trust in you, Lord, I say, "You are my God." My days are in your hand... smile on your servant, save me in your love.

Psalm 31:14–16

About the Author

Catherine Kolyschkine was born into a wealthy family in Russia on the feast of the Assumption, August 15, 1896 (N.S.). She was baptized in the Russian Orthodox Church, although many Christian strands were woven into the spiritual fabric of her family, including Catholicism. During her father's long assignments abroad in connection with Russian diplomatic and business interests, Catherine was entrusted to convent schools and Catholic nuns. However, the distinctively Russian incarnation of the Gospel was the great crucible into which every other element poured to forge Catherine's early life.

From the liturgy of the Russian Orthodox Church, the living faith of her father and mother, and the earthy piety of the Russian people themselves, sinners and skeptics as well as saints, she received the powerful spiritual traditions and symbols of the Christian East.

At fifteen Catherine was married to Boris de Hueck. Soon they were swept into the devastating battles of World War I, she as a nurse, he as an engineer. After the Revolution of 1917, they endured with all the peoples of the Russian Empire the agonies of starvation and civil war. Many of Catherine's relatives were killed, but she and Boris escaped at last and, stripped of everything but clothes and faith, made their way to Finland and then to England.

It was in England that Catherine formally became a Roman Catholic. At the beginning of her new life in the West, Catherine accepted the teachings of the Catholic Church, without rejecting, then or ever, the spiritual wealth of her Orthodox heritage.

In 1921, Boris and Catherine, with little money and uncertain health, sailed to Canada. She was pregnant and gave birth to her son, George, soon after they arrived in their new country. They settled in Toronto, but even with the help of friends it was not easy to find work that would support them and their child. Catherine often remembered that she had first come to know the people of North America not through wealthy benefactors who were intrigued by her aristocratic connections, but in the working poor whose lives she shared as maid, laundress, waitress and salesclerk.

Soon Catherine's intelligence, energy, and gift for public speaking brought her to the attention of a large lecture bureau. Her talks were popular all across Canada and the United States. Within a few years, she became an executive with another, international lecture service. Before long she had a large apartment, many books, a nurse for her son, a fine car, celebrated friends. She was a North American success story.

But Catherine began to wonder. Her marriage was disintegrating, and she seemed unable to heal it. Moreover, she knew that she was also struggling with God. Had He saved her from death in Russia so many times only to make her a comfortable bourgeoise in North America?

The words of Christ haunted her: "Sell all you possess, and give it to the poor, and come, follow me." It seemed madness, and she tried to close her soul to these words, which she has described as sounding within her like the faint, disjointed stammering of a dying man. She could not escape them.

In the early 1930s, after several years of anguish, Catherine and Boris separated permanently; later, the Church annulled their marriage. As devastated as Catherine was by what felt to her yet another, more intimate death, she knew that God wanted something new from her now. But she did not know what it was.

It was to the Archbishop of Toronto, Neil McNeil, that she turned for help in her need for a word from the Lord. The Archbishop listened to Catherine and told her that he believed God was asking something most unusual from her, something that would demand her own crucifixion on the other side of the cross of Christ. Did she love Christ enough to do that?

Catherine did. She agreed to spend a year in prayer for further discernment, and when the year was over, the Archbishop gave Catherine his blessing, and she and her son went to live in a humble section of the city. George was enrolled in a good school, and Catherine began to seek to obey the Lord's word to her "to become one with the poor, one with Him."

At first Catherine desired only to be with the poor, to love and serve them very quietly, to become their friend, to pray with them, hidden in their midst. But when others saw her and heard her speak, they wanted to join her. There was an intensity to her faith and love that lit a flame in the hearts of many men and women. Catherine had not envisaged a community, but when the Archbishop told her that, yes, Christ was calling her to found a community of lay people to serve him in the poor, she accepted what he said. Soon Friendship House was born.

The works of Friendship House were modest—a shelter for the homeless, meals for the hungry, recreation and books for the young, a newspaper to make known the social teachings of the Church. The prophetic voice of Catherine and the community of Friendship House resounded boldly, however, in a city where Catholics were not well accepted. The poor welcomed her, but others were scandalized by her forceful insistence that caring for the poor was not optional for Christians. After a few years, misunderstanding and gossip drove her out of Toronto. The first Friendship House was dead.

Yet Catherine's voice had reached other ears in North America. In 1938 Father John LaFarge, S.J., arranged to have the Archbishop of New York invite her to work in Harlem. She agreed to start Friendship House again, alone, in total poverty, this time among the African-Americans. Catherine brought them not only compassion and an irresistible passion for justice, but her whole soul.

Once again men and women came to share her life and work. The interracial apostolate grew in New York and expanded to other cities, to Chicago, Washington D.C., and Portland, Oregon. Friendship House became well known, if not necessarily well thought of, in the American Church. Catherine shared with her friend Dorothy Day of the Catholic Worker, the intense struggle to move the gospel out of books into believers' lives. Even if a few, such as the young Thomas Merton, recognized in her the power of the Holy Spirit and an unwavering fidelity to Christ's Church, many others were frightened by her Russian bluntness. Others simply could not grasp the largeness of her vision, especially because her experience of the ways of God were so foreign to them. Finally after a painful difference of opinion over the nature of the Friendship House apostolate, Catherine found herself pushed again into the chartless waters of the Lord.

This time, however, Catherine did not have to start alone. In 1943, she had married Eddie Doherty, a celebrated newspaperman, after he convinced her and her bishop that he wanted to share and support her vocation. In 1947, then, Catherine and Eddie came to Combermere, a small village 180 miles northeast of Toronto, where the

Bishop of Pembroke had agreed she could work among the rural families.

They came bewildered and uncertain. Still exhausted with grief of another separation, they planted a dozen apple trees. Somehow they knew that they had come home, and that the mysterious vocation of prayer, communal love and simple service of the poor, which the Lord had given to Catherine, would not be lost. They could not see what the future held, and often during the first years in Combermere they were tempted to leave. But they had planted those trees, and if they had come to what seemed to them a wilderness, they knew that it was the Lord's and that he would make it bloom.

He did. Again others came to join Catherine, and this time priests came to stay as well. The apostolate, now called Madonna House, grew slowly. Father John T. Callahan, the founder-director of the priests of Madonna House, was a constant support.

In 1955, when the community had agreed to establish itself more formally in the Church with vows of poverty, chastity and obedience leading to a life-time commitment, Catherine and Eddie took a vow of celibacy. Their sacrifice bore fruit in vocations and in stability, and in 1978 Bishop Joseph R. Windle approved the constitution of Madonna House as a single community with branches of laymen, laywomen and clerics. (Under the new code of canon law, the apostolate is a Public Association of the Christian Faithful.)

At present, over fifty years later, Madonna House has more than 200 members, including twenty priests, and more than 100 associate priests. The apostolate has missions in Belgium, England, Ghana, Russia, and more than a dozen others in Canada and the United States.

The training center in Combermere offers an experience of the Gospel life to hundreds every year.

As Catherine's inner life deepened and the community matured, she was better able to share with us the fullness of the inner vocation Christ had formed in her through the many blessings and struggles of her life. "Love is ingenious", she liked to say, and the ingenuity of her heart and her mind found new words and deeds to show us how deep and how broad was the call Madonna House had received through her "to restore all things in Christ."

Fr. Robert Pelton
Madonna House Apostolate

More information about Catherine Doherty's life, works, and news about the progress of her cause for canonization as a saint can be found at the Internet web site: **www.catherinedoherty.org**

Books by Catherine Doherty

Apostolic Farming: Healing the Earth
Beginning Again: Recovering Your Joy Through Confession
Bogoroditza: She Who Gave Birth to God
Dear Father: A Message of Love for Priests
Dear Seminarian: On Becoming a Shepherd of Souls
Donkey Bells: Advent and Christmas
An Experience of God: Identification with Christ
Fragments of My Life: A Memoir
God in the Nitty-Gritty Life: The Gospel in Everyday Life
Grace in Every Season
In the Footprints of Loneliness
In the Furnace of Doubts
Living the Gospel Without Compromise
Molchanie: Experiencing the Silence of God
My Russian Yesterdays
Not Without Parables: Tales of Yesterday, Today & Eternity
On the Cross of Rejection
Poustinia: Encountering God in Silence, Solitude and Prayer
Season of Mercy: Lent and Easter
Sobornost: Experiencing Unity of Mind, Heart and Soul
Soul of My Soul: Coming to the Heart of Prayer
The Stations of the Cross: In the Footsteps of the Passion
Strannik: The Call to the Pilgrimage of the Heart
Urodivoi: Holy Fools

Available from **Madonna House Publications**
Toll free phone: **1-888-703-7110**
Internet: **www.madonnahouse.org/publications**
2888 Dafoe Rd, Combermere, Ontario, Canada K0J 1L0

Madonna House Publications
www.madonnahouse.org/publications

"Lord, give bread to the hungry, and hunger for you to those who have bread," was a favourite prayer of our foundress, Catherine Doherty. At Madonna House Publications, we strive to satisfy the spiritual hunger for God in our modern world with the timeless words of the Gospel message.

Faithful to the teachings of the Catholic Church and its magisterium, Madonna House Publications is a non-profit apostolate dedicated to publishing high quality and easily accessible books, audiobooks, videos and music. We pray our publications will awaken and deepen in our readers an experience of Jesus' love in the most simple and ordinary facets of everyday life.

Your generosity can help Madonna House Publications provide the poor around the world with editions of important spiritual works containing the enduring wisdom of the Gospel message. If you would like to help, please send your contribution to the address below. We also welcome your questions and comments. May God bless you for your participation in this apostolate.

Madonna House Publications
2888 Dafoe Rd
Combermere ON   K0J 1L0
Canada

Internet: www.madonnahouse.org/publications
E-mail: publications@madonnahouse.org
Telephone: 613-756-3728